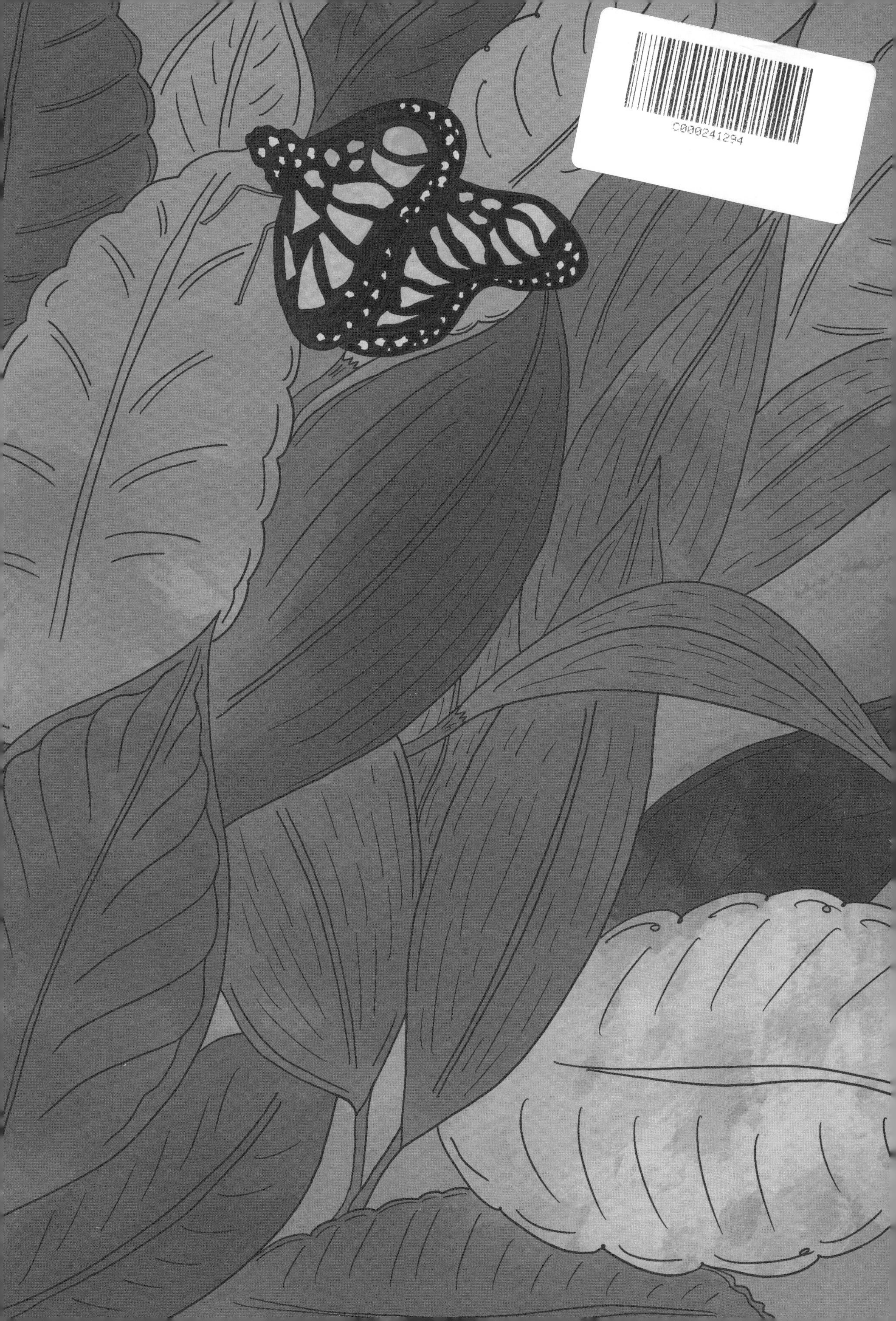

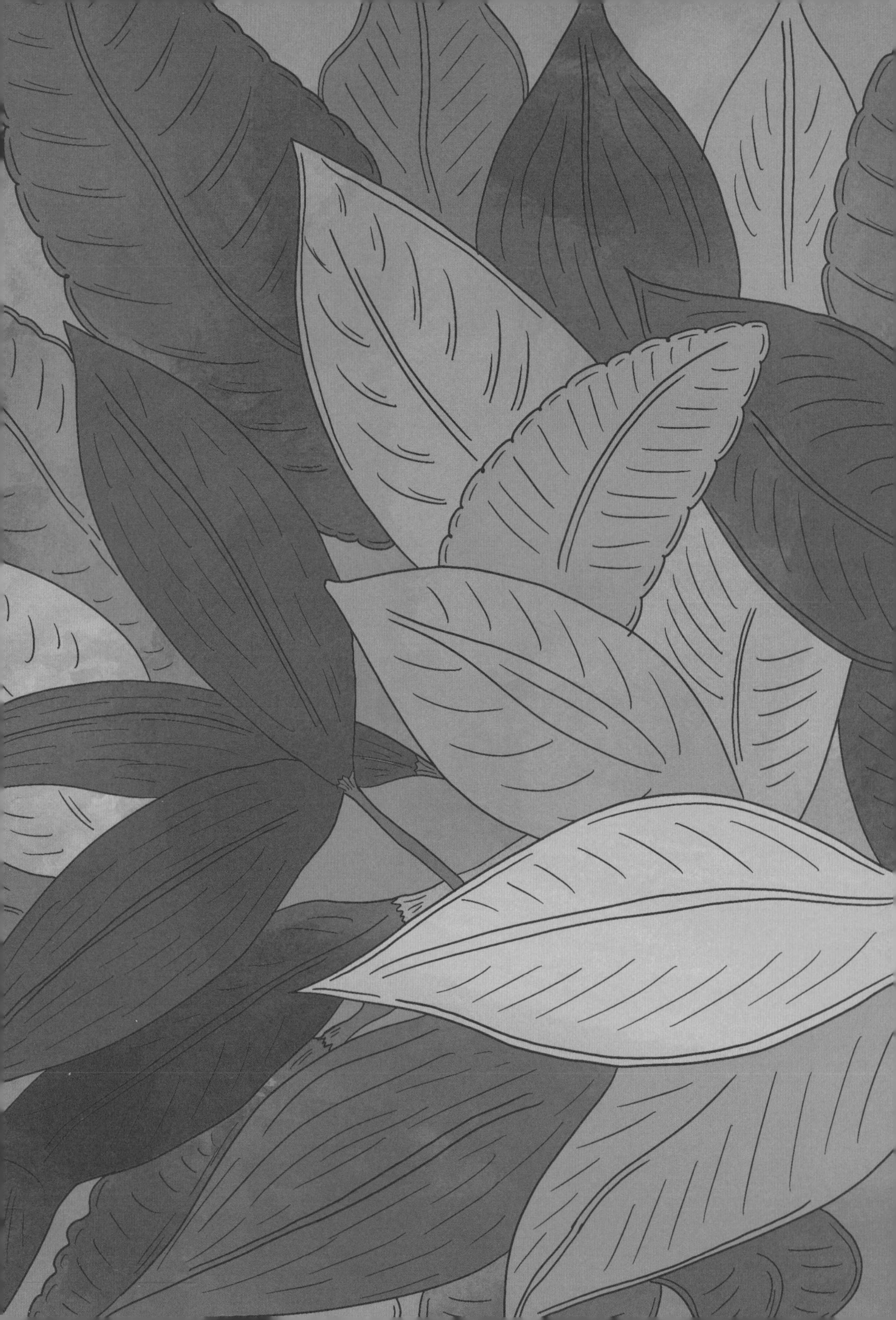

# FRIDA KAHLO

## HER LIFE, HER WORK, HER HOME

FIRST PUBLISHED IN 2023
BY SELFMADEHERO
139–141 PANCRAS ROAD
LONDON NW1 1UN
WWW.SELFMADEHERO.COM

COPYRIGHT © 2023
FRANCISCO DE LA MORA/SARA AFONSO
FOREWORD © CIRCE HENESTROSA

SCRIPT & ILLUSTRATIONS: FRANCISCO DE LA MORA
TRANSLATION: LAWRENCE SCHIMEL
TYPEFACE CREATED BY OLIVIER KUGLER
PUBLISHING DIRECTOR: EMMA HAYLEY
TEXTUAL CONSULTANT: NICK DE SOMOGYI
PUBLICIST: PAUL SMITH
DIGITAL CONTENT MANAGER: STEFANO MANCIN
WITH THANKS TO TXABI JONES

IMAGES ON PAGES:
14-15-27-28-30-31-32-35-45-51-57-58-59-60-61
© 2021, BANCO DE MÉXICO,
DIEGO RIVERA & FRIDA KAHLO MUSEUMS TRUST.
AV. 5 DE MAYO NO. 2, COL. CENTRO, ALC. CUAUHTÉMOC,
C.P. 06000, MEXICO CITY.

A CIP RECORD FOR THIS BOOK IS AVAILABLE FROM THE BRITISH LIBRARY

ISBN: 978-1-914224-10-2

10 9 8 7 6 5 4 3 2 1

PRINTED AND BOUND IN THE UK

# FRIDA KAHLO

## HER LIFE, HER WORK, HER HOME

BY FRANCISCO DE LA MORA
TRANSLATED BY LAWRENCE SCHIMEL

SELF
MADE
HERO

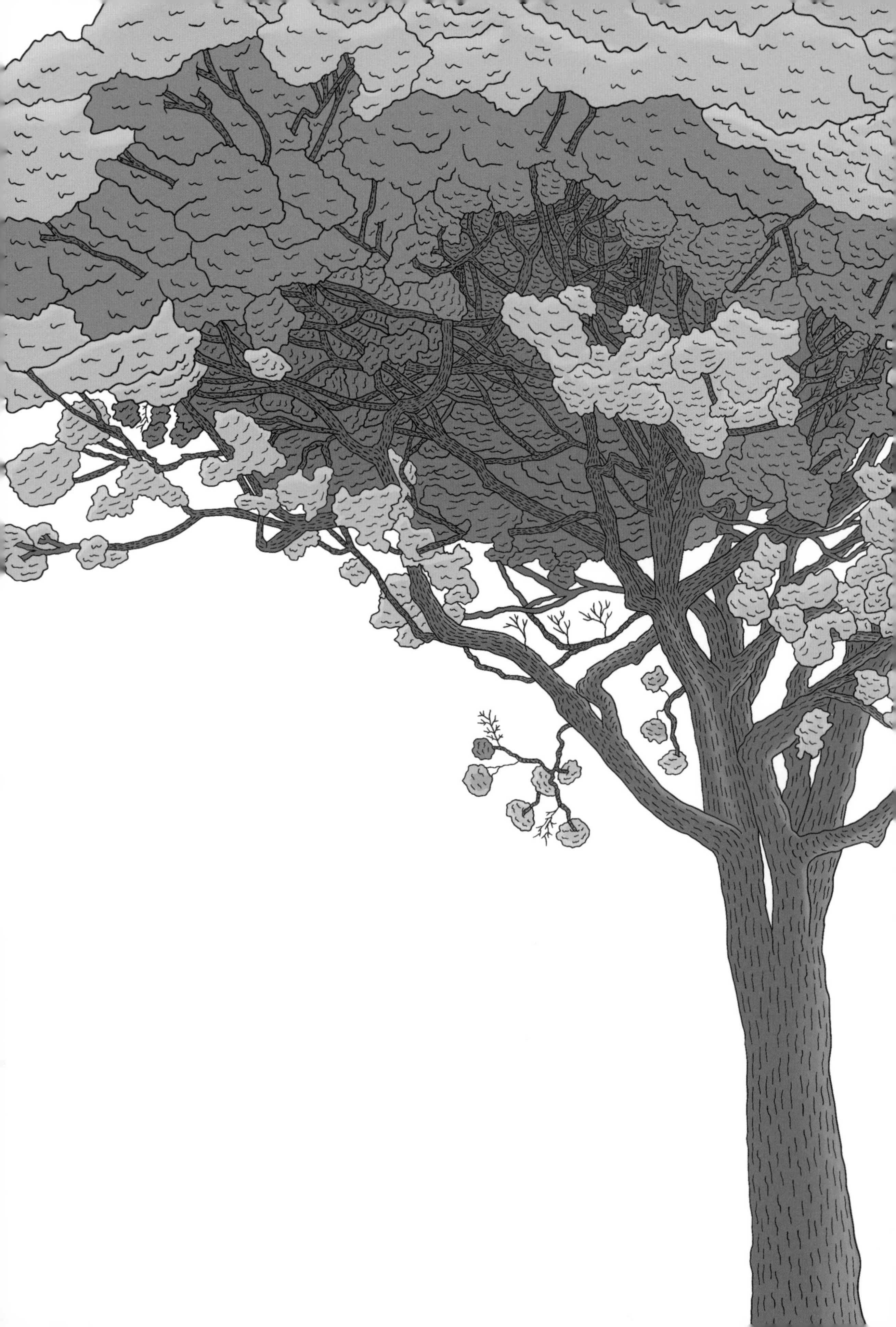

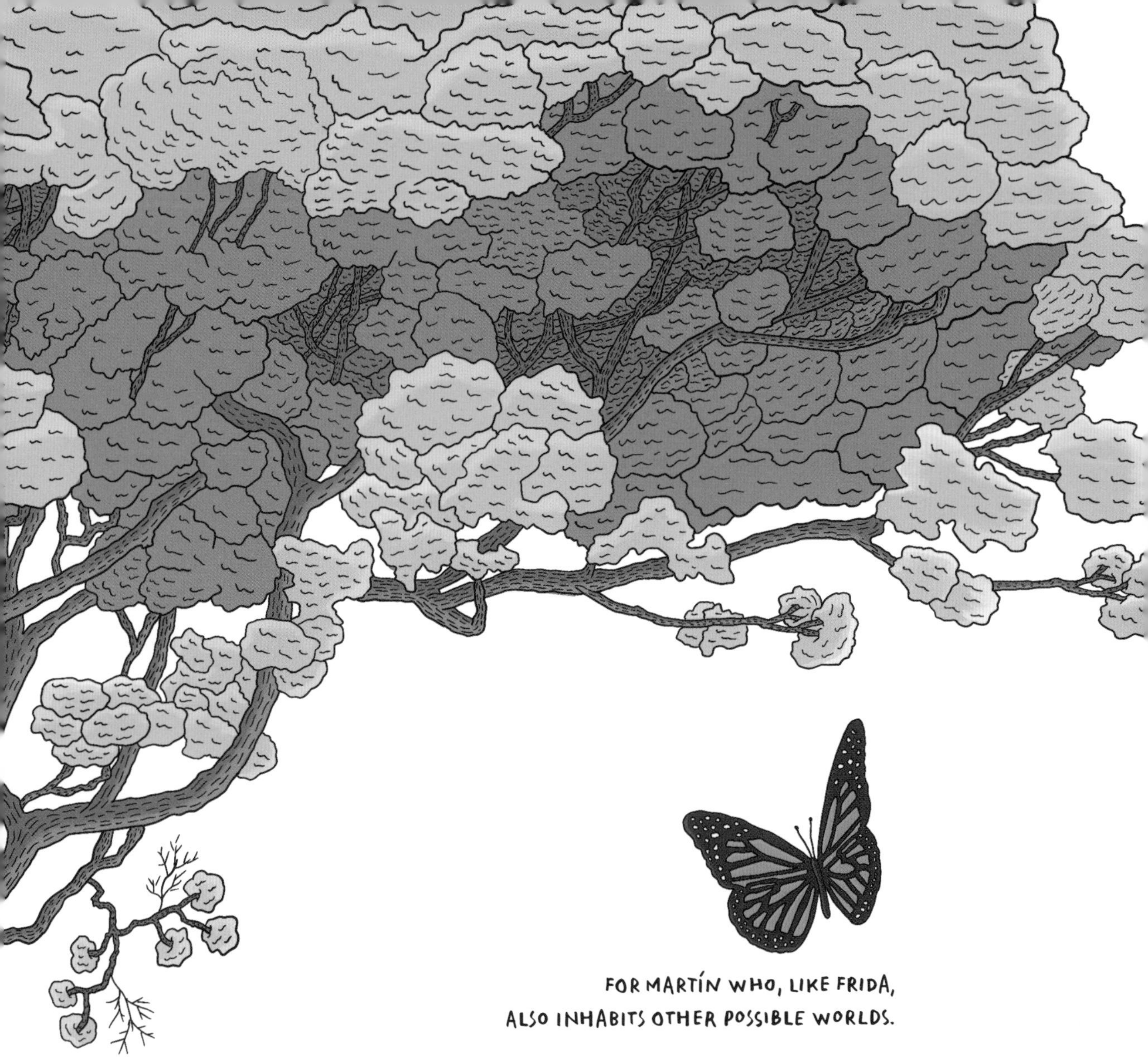

FOR MARTÍN WHO, LIKE FRIDA,
ALSO INHABITS OTHER POSSIBLE WORLDS.

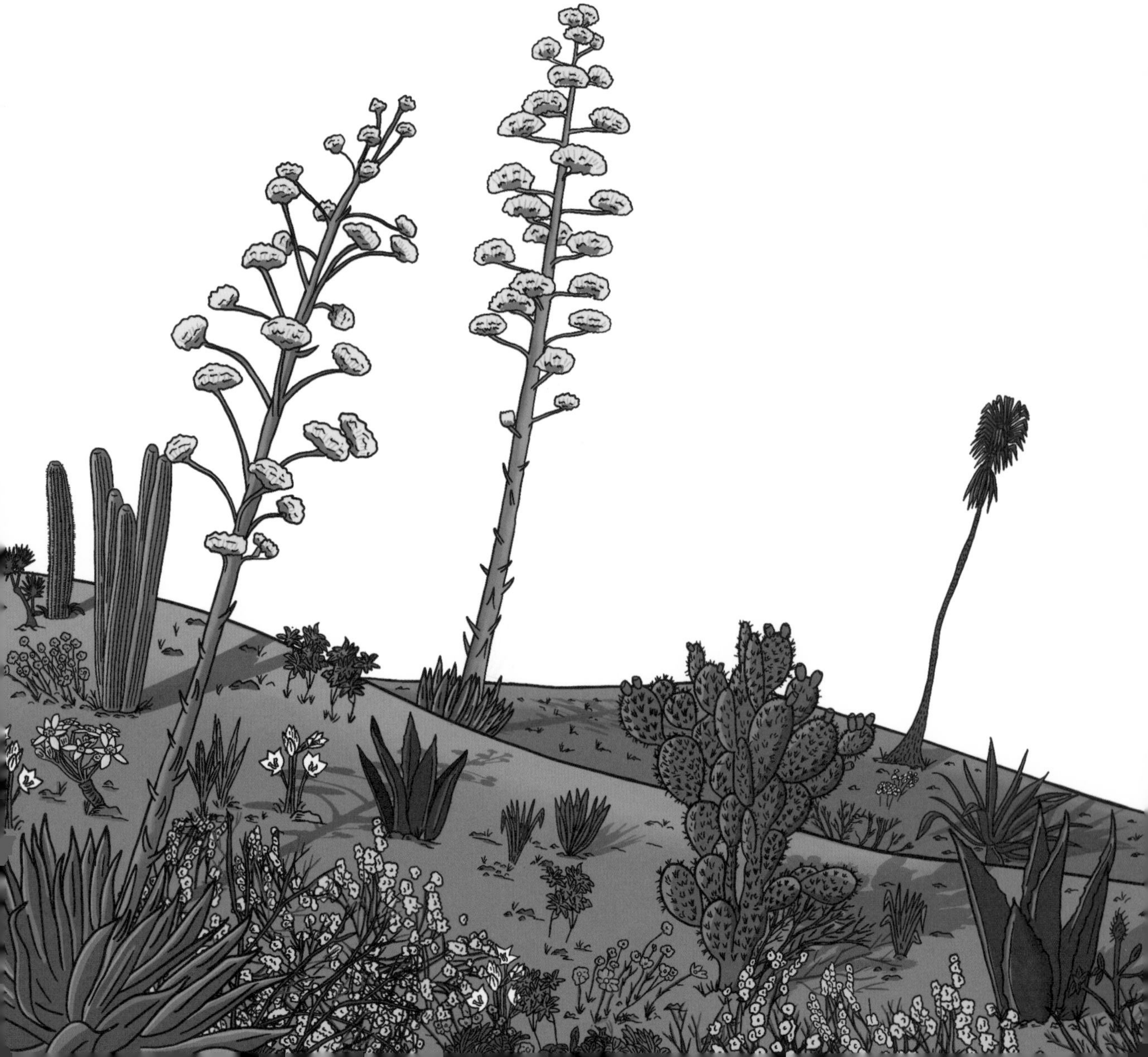

# FOREWORD

Dear friends,

My name is Circe Henestrosa, and I am an educator and a fashion curator. I am so happy to be here with you to share this amazing graphic novel created by Mexican artist and illustrator Francisco de la Mora. When Francisco asked me to write an introduction for this wonderful story he has drawn and written with so much care and love for all of us, I was thrilled. *Frida Kahlo: Her Life, Her Work, Her Home* is a beautiful piece of art.

Francisco and I grew up hearing many stories about Frida Kahlo back in our native country, Mexico. We even visited the house where she was born, lived, and died: the Blue House – today the Frida Kahlo Museum. We both feel a very special connection to Frida Kahlo, our Mexican traditions, and our native Mexico. I will share with you my own personal connection to Frida. My family on my father's side come from the Tehuantepec Isthmus, located in the southeast part of Mexico in Oaxaca, where women are in charge and dress in the ethnically colourful and beautiful Tehuana attire. This dress was popularized by Frida Kahlo and is the one we all now know as hers. My aunt Alfa, an indigenous woman from Tehuantepec and a good friend to Frida, gave her some of her first Tehuana dresses when she decided to adopt this garment as her signature look. Frida was so proud of her Mexican roots, and the Mexican people, that she wanted to distinguish herself as an indigenous woman. This dress not only allowed her to look indigenous – and look like a queen – but also helped her deal with her physical disabilities. At the same time she distinguished herself as a female artist in a period when the art world was dominated by men.

Most people don't know that Kahlo was disabled at different stages of her life. At the age of six, she suffered from polio, leaving her right leg shorter than her left. She started wearing two or three socks on one foot to level them out, and took to dressing in long skirts to cover her legs. At the age of 18 she suffered a terrible accident while on her way home from school, when the bus she was travelling in collided with a tram, and a metal bar pierced her body. It is due to this accident, and the time Frida spent in bed recovering from it, that she became an artist. At that time, her mother installed a mirror under the canopy of her four-poster bed for Frida to see herself in while painting her self-portraits. She would conceal her body underneath beautiful fabrics, but at the same time reveal her body through her art.

Frida's life was short. She was born on 6 July 1907 and died on 13 July 1954. At the age of 22 she met, fell in love with, and married the Mexican artist Diego Rivera. Kahlo first travelled outside Mexico shortly after her marriage, accompanying Rivera to "Gringolandia", as she called the United States. He was already a celebrated artist, commissioned to paint murals in San Francisco, New York, and Detroit. Frida's encounters in the United States (1930–33) were complex and impactful. In San Francisco, she fashioned her singular Tehuana style, made lifelong friends, was photographed by brilliant photographers, and began painting seriously. She enjoyed exploring "magical" New York, but criticized the wealth gap and racism she observed. In Detroit, a traumatic miscarriage radically transformed her art, and she reinvented herself as the painter we know today. (This was a central feature of 'Frida Kahlo: Appearances Can Be Deceiving', an exhibition I curated, with Gannit Ankori, at San Francisco's de Young Museum in 2020.)

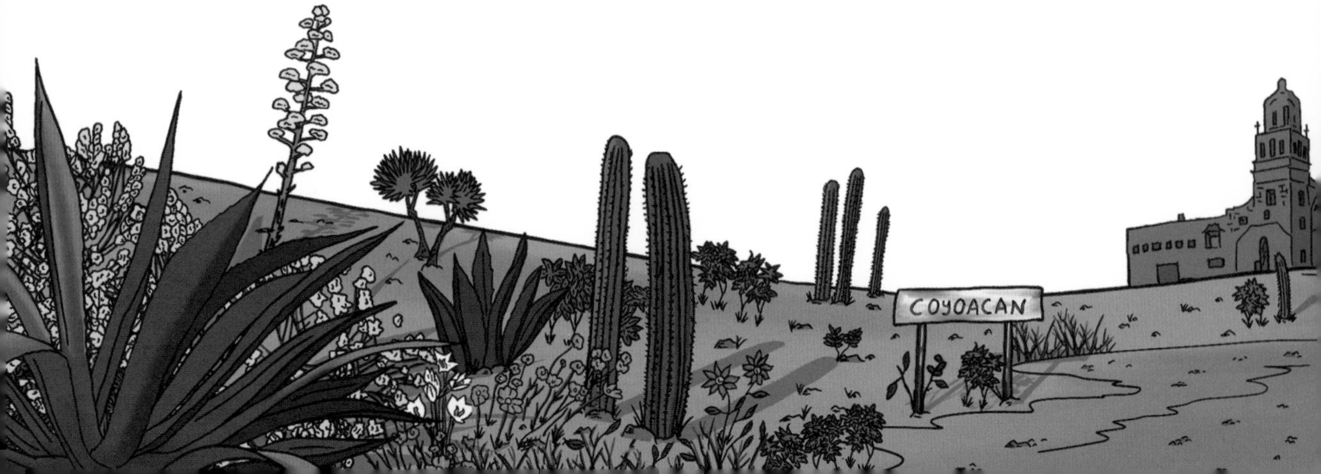
COYOACAN

Frida had her first solo exhibition as an artist at the Julien Levy Gallery in New York in 1938, then travelled to Paris in 1939 to present her work there, where she was internationally recognized. In 1953, just months before her death, her friend Lola Álvarez, a famous Mexican photographer, organized Frida's first solo exhibition in Mexico. Through her self-portraits, and the use of traditional Mexican dresses to style herself, Kahlo dealt with her life, health struggles, turbulent marriage, and the accident that meant she could never have children.

Today Frida Kahlo is considered one of the most important Mexican artists. Her work has been celebrated internationally as representative of Mexican national and indigenous traditions, and for depicting the female experience and form. Her image and art endure because she was able to break so many taboos about women's experiences, and about the challenges of overcoming illness and physical injury, working through trauma in creative ways. Her resilience, fighting attitude, and determination to enjoy life despite all the obstacles she encountered make her a powerful symbol as she continues to speak to all of us. Her iconic image communicates indomitable strength and the constant possibility of change.

Through these pages, Francisco de la Mora has skilfully illustrated the life and work of this wonderful and inspirational Mexican artist. I hope she continues impacting your life as much as she has impacted ours.

Enjoy!

Circe Henestrosa
*Head of the School of Fashion,*
*LASALLE College of the Arts, Singapore*

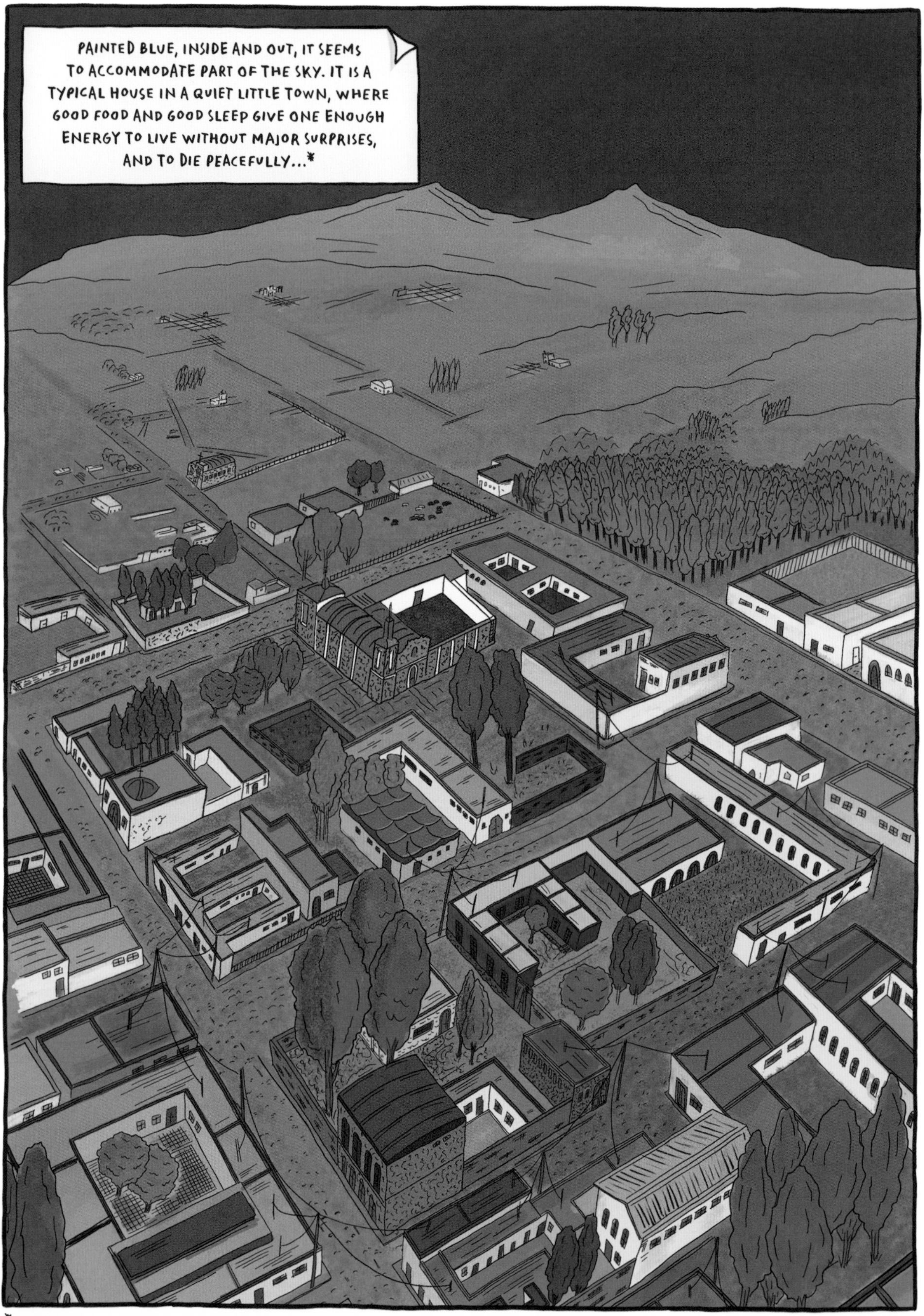
PAINTED BLUE, INSIDE AND OUT, IT SEEMS TO ACCOMMODATE PART OF THE SKY. IT IS A TYPICAL HOUSE IN A QUIET LITTLE TOWN, WHERE GOOD FOOD AND GOOD SLEEP GIVE ONE ENOUGH ENERGY TO LIVE WITHOUT MAJOR SURPRISES, AND TO DIE PEACEFULLY...*

* CARLOS PELLICER (POET AND FRIDA'S FRIEND).

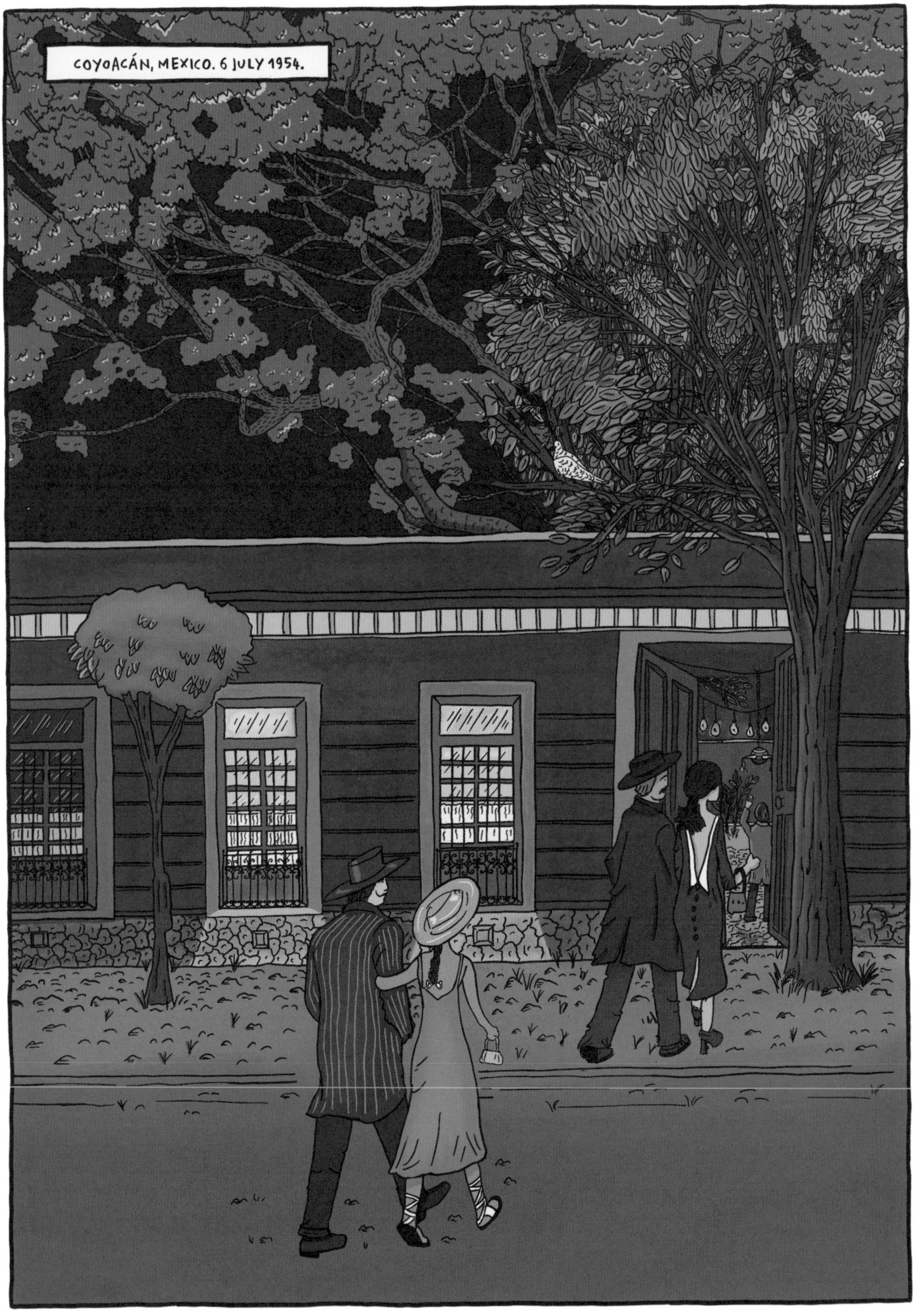
COYOACÁN, MEXICO. 6 JULY 1954.

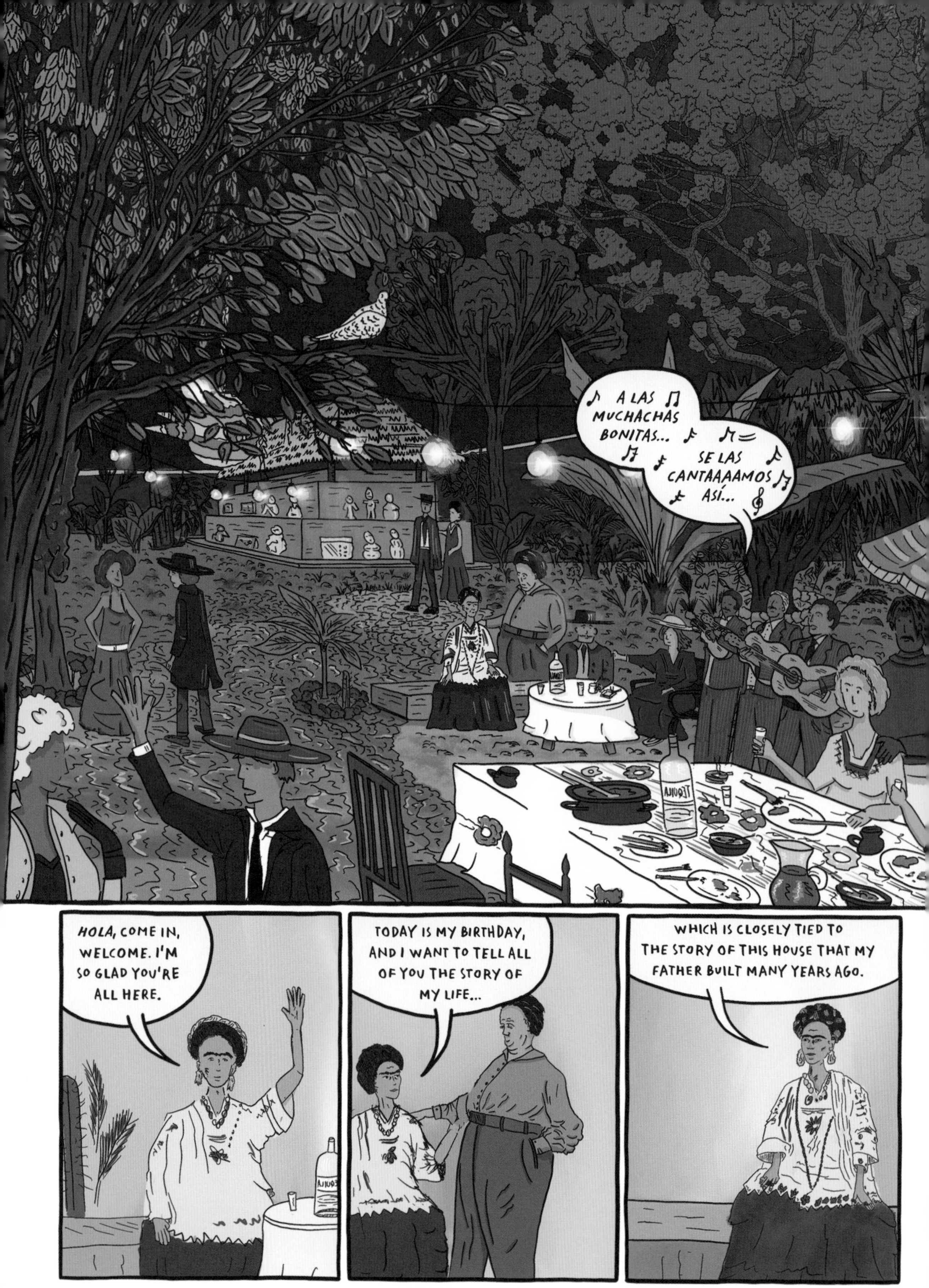
A LAS MUCHACHAS BONITAS...
SE LAS CANTAAAAMOS ASÍ...
TEQUILA
HOLA, COME IN, WELCOME. I'M SO GLAD YOU'RE ALL HERE.
TODAY IS MY BIRTHDAY, AND I WANT TO TELL ALL OF YOU THE STORY OF MY LIFE...
WHICH IS CLOSELY TIED TO THE STORY OF THIS HOUSE THAT MY FATHER BUILT MANY YEARS AGO.

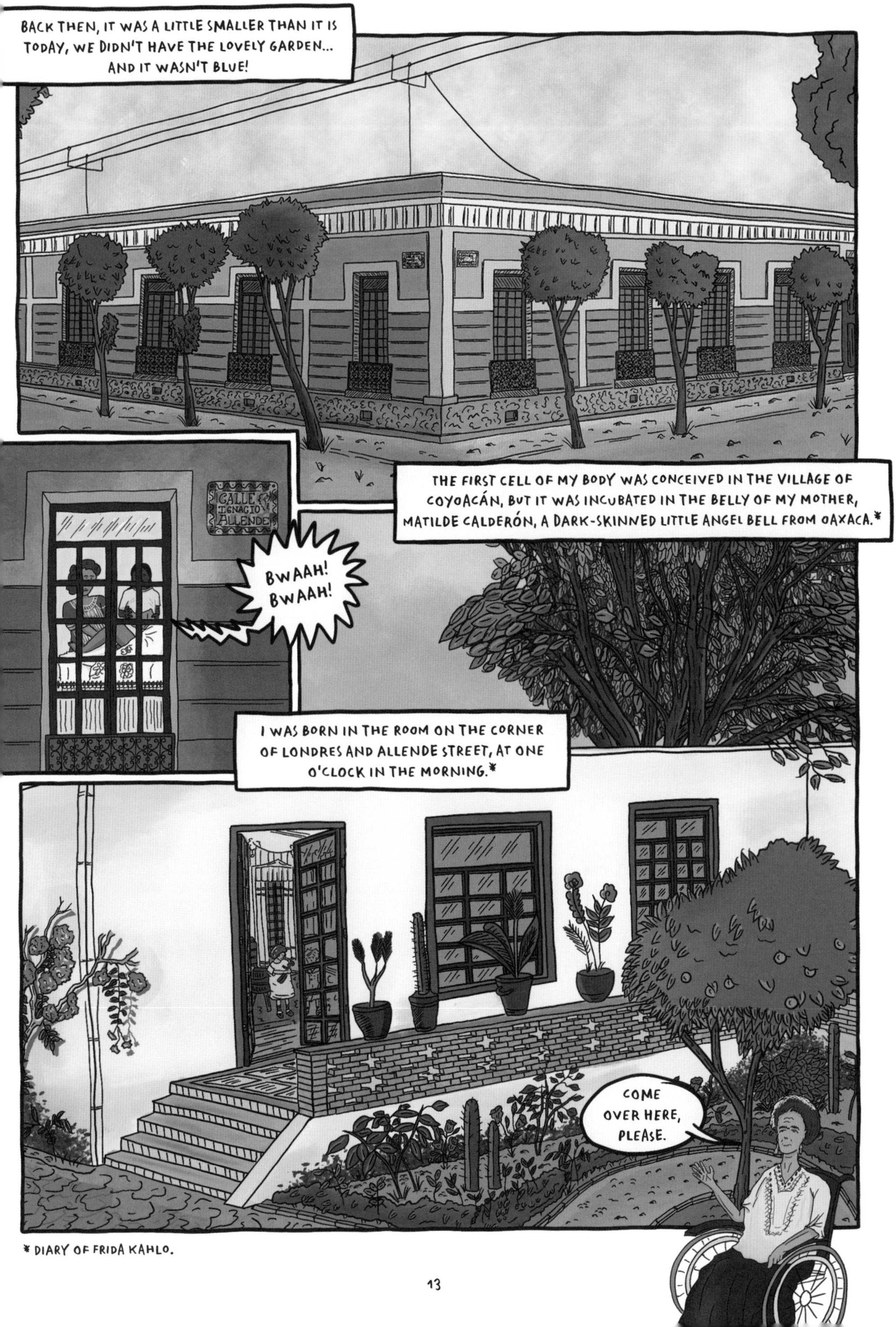
BACK THEN, IT WAS A LITTLE SMALLER THAN IT IS TODAY, WE DIDN'T HAVE THE LOVELY GARDEN... AND IT WASN'T BLUE!
CALLE IGNACIO ALLENDE
THE FIRST CELL OF MY BODY WAS CONCEIVED IN THE VILLAGE OF COYOACÁN, BUT IT WAS INCUBATED IN THE BELLY OF MY MOTHER, MATILDE CALDERÓN, A DARK-SKINNED LITTLE ANGEL BELL FROM OAXACA.*
BWAAH! BWAAH!
I WAS BORN IN THE ROOM ON THE CORNER OF LONDRES AND ALLENDE STREET, AT ONE O'CLOCK IN THE MORNING.*
COME OVER HERE, PLEASE.

* DIARY OF FRIDA KAHLO.

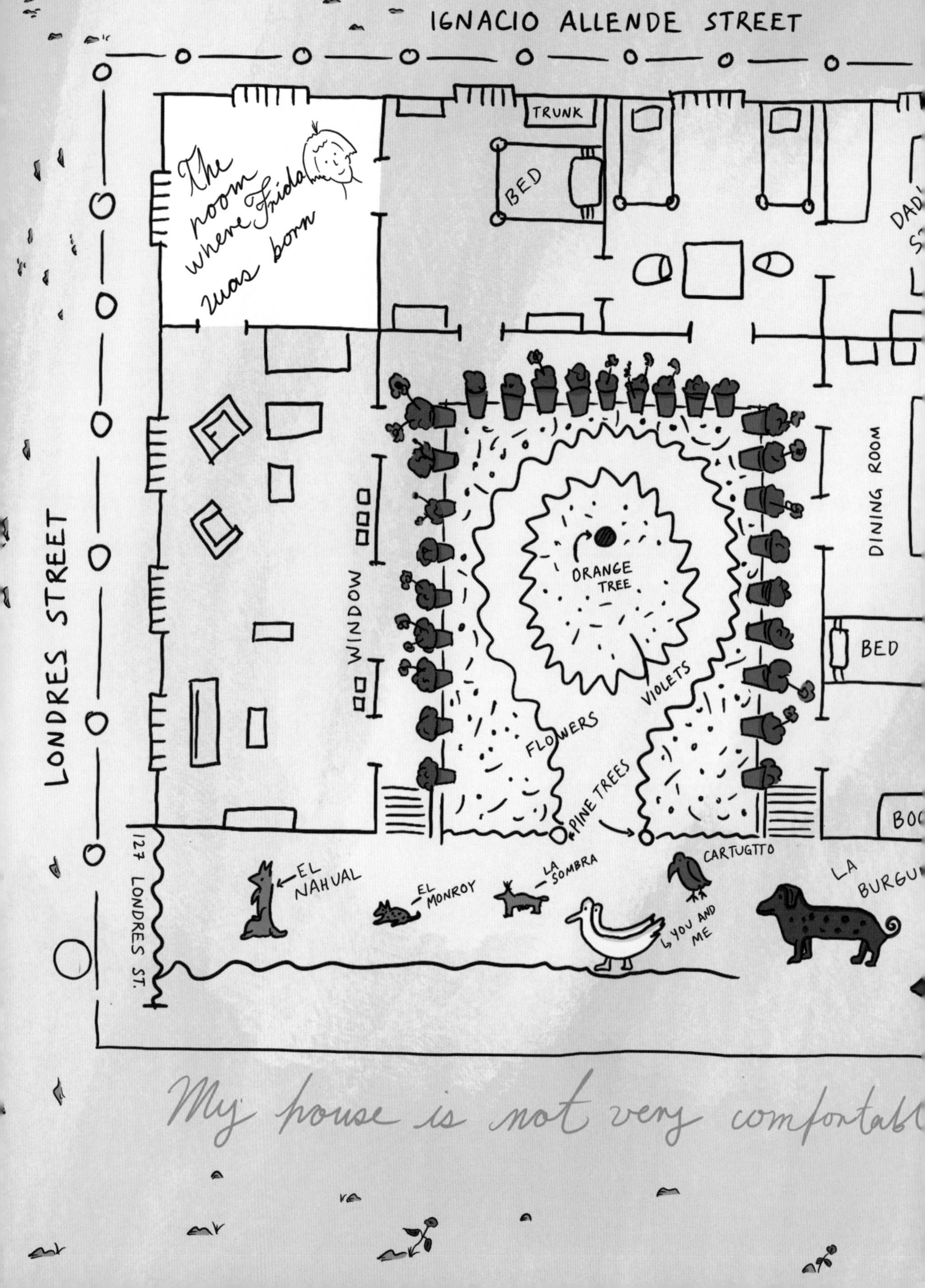
IGNACIO ALLENDE STREET
TRUNK
BED
The room where Frida was born
LONDRES STREET
WINDOW
ORANGE TREE
VIOLETS
FLOWERS
PINE TREES
DINING ROOM
BED
127 LONDRES ST.
EL NAHUAL
EL MONROY
LA SOMBRA
CARTUGTTO
YOU AND ME

My house is not very comfortabl

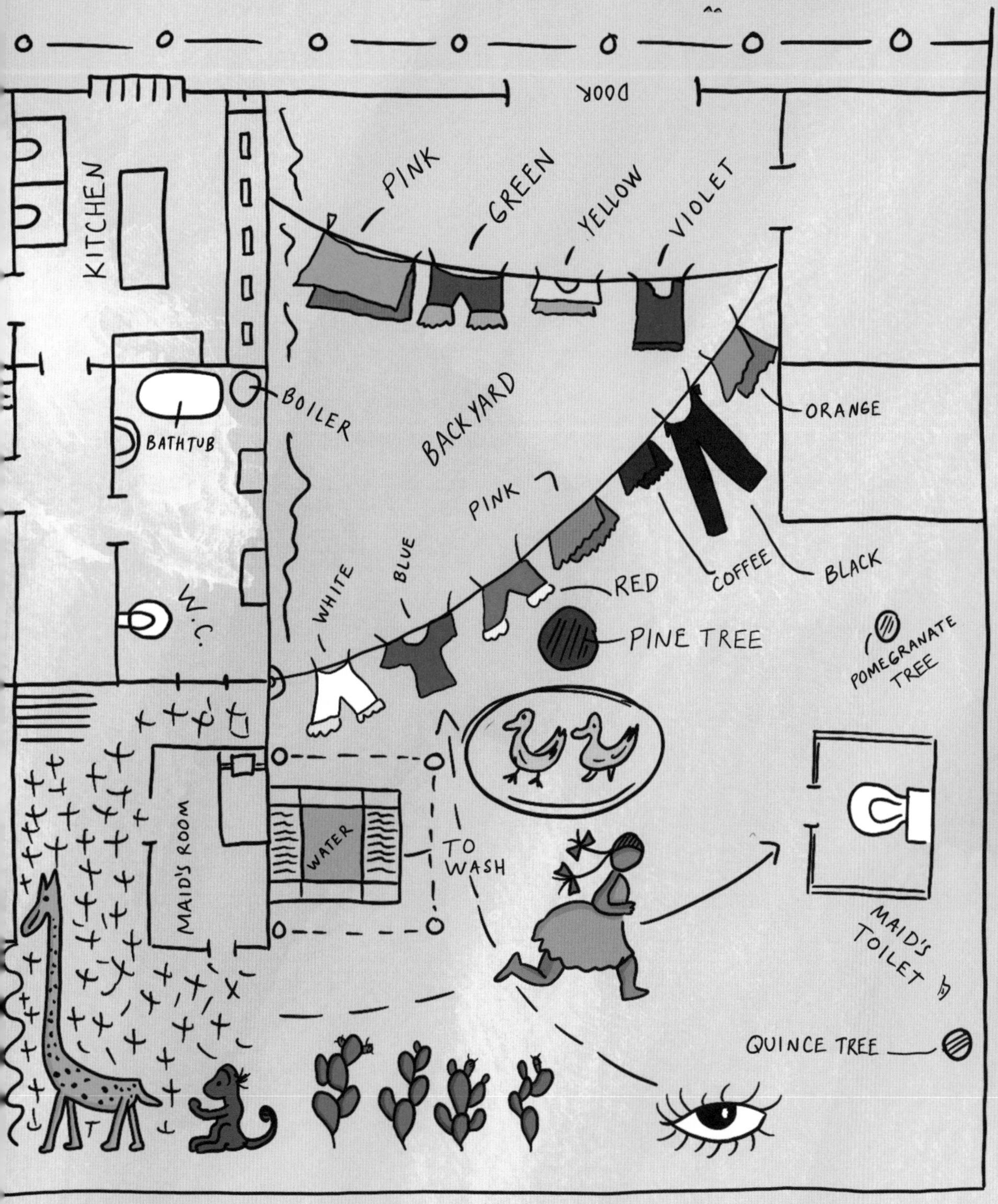
DOOR
KITCHEN
PINK
GREEN
YELLOW
VIOLET
BOILER
BATHTUB
BACKYARD
ORANGE
PINK
W.C.
WHITE
BLUE
RED
COFFEE
BLACK
PINE TREE
POMEGRANATE TREE
MAID'S ROOM
WATER
TO WASH
MAID'S TOILET
QUINCE TREE

ut it has nice colours

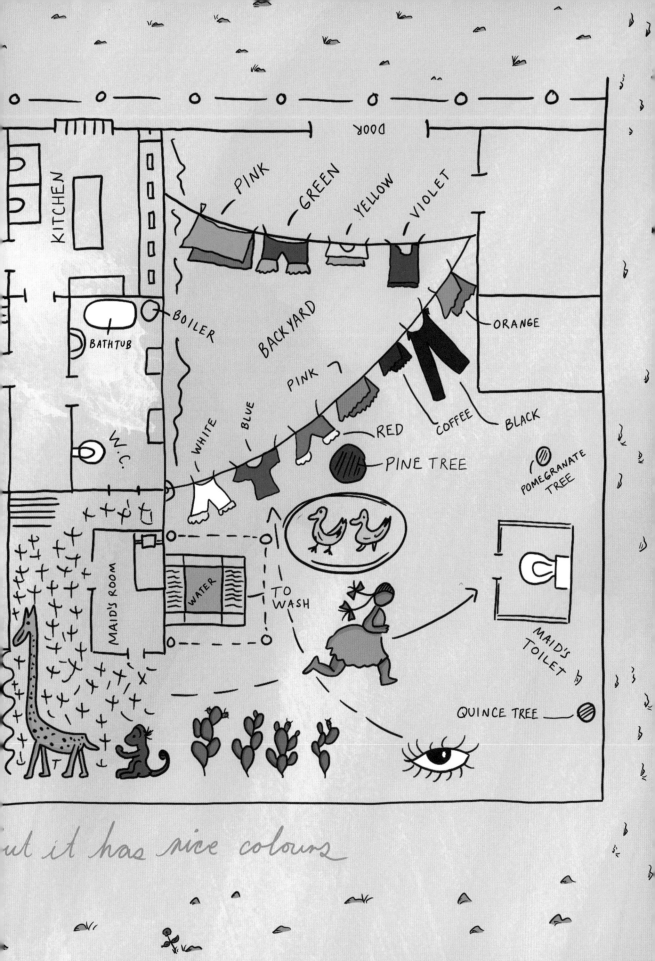

MY CHILDHOOD WAS WONDERFUL...

PAPÁ

LUISA    MARGARITA

MAMÁ

FRIDA    CRIS

ADRIANA    MATILDE

... BECAUSE MY FATHER, WHO WAS A PHOTOGRAPHER AS WELL AS A PAINTER, SET A TREMENDOUS EXAMPLE TO ME OF KINDNESS AND HARD WORK. *

GUILLERMO KAHLO — THAT WAS HIS NAME — WAS BORN IN GERMANY, AND EMIGRATED TO MEXICO IN THE 19TH CENTURY.

HE MARRIED A MEXICAN *SEÑORITA*, MOTHER OF MY TWO HALF-SISTERS, LUISA AND MARGARITA.

WHEN HIS WIFE DIED VERY YOUNG, MY FATHER MARRIED MY MOTHER, MATILDE CALDERÓN Y GONZÁLEZ, A SERIOUS AND LOVELY WOMAN.

MATILDE HAD FOUR DAUGHTERS: MATITA, ADRI, ME (FRIDA), AND DEAR, PUDGY LITTLE CRISTI. *

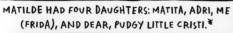

* DIARY OF FRIDA KAHLO.

I ALWAYS HAD A SPECIAL RELATIONSHIP WITH CRISTINA.

SHE WAS THE STEADIEST PRESENCE IN MY LIFE.

I REMEMBER MY EARLY YEARS AS A TIME OF JOY AND PEACE. MY FATHER WORKED AS A PHOTOGRAPHER FOR THE PORFIRIO DÍAZ GOVERNMENT, AND WE LIVED WITHOUT MAJOR ECONOMIC WORRIES.

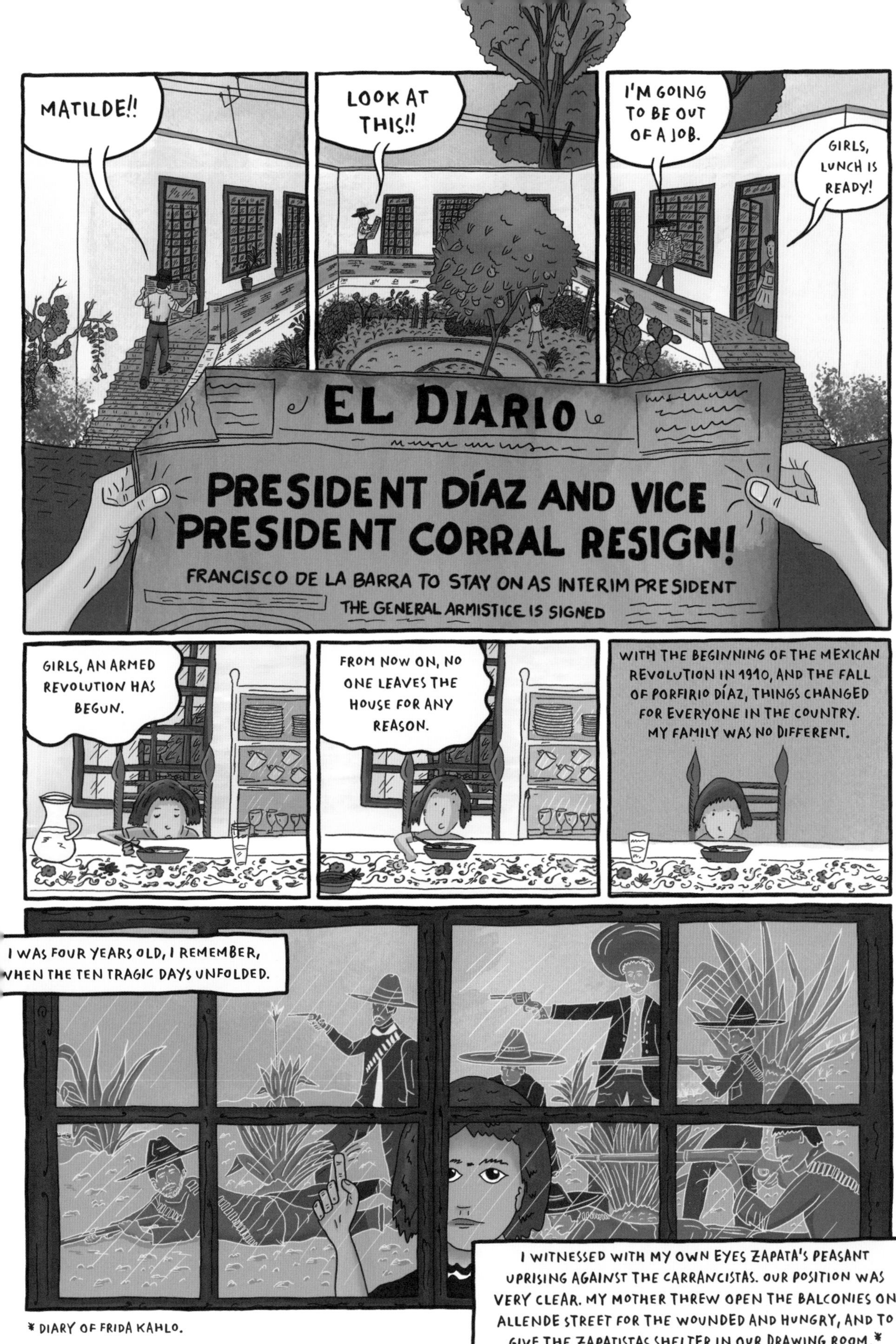

MATILDE!!
LOOK AT THIS!!
I'M GOING TO BE OUT OF A JOB.
GIRLS, LUNCH IS READY!
EL DIARIO
PRESIDENT DÍAZ AND VICE PRESIDENT CORRAL RESIGN!
FRANCISCO DE LA BARRA TO STAY ON AS INTERIM PRESIDENT
THE GENERAL ARMISTICE IS SIGNED
GIRLS, AN ARMED REVOLUTION HAS BEGUN.
FROM NOW ON, NO ONE LEAVES THE HOUSE FOR ANY REASON.
WITH THE BEGINNING OF THE MEXICAN REVOLUTION IN 1910, AND THE FALL OF PORFIRIO DÍAZ, THINGS CHANGED FOR EVERYONE IN THE COUNTRY. MY FAMILY WAS NO DIFFERENT.
I WAS FOUR YEARS OLD, I REMEMBER, WHEN THE TEN TRAGIC DAYS UNFOLDED.
I WITNESSED WITH MY OWN EYES ZAPATA'S PEASANT UPRISING AGAINST THE CARRANCISTAS. OUR POSITION WAS VERY CLEAR. MY MOTHER THREW OPEN THE BALCONIES ON ALLENDE STREET FOR THE WOUNDED AND HUNGRY, AND TO GIVE THE ZAPATISTAS SHELTER IN OUR DRAWING ROOM.*


* DIARY OF FRIDA KAHLO.

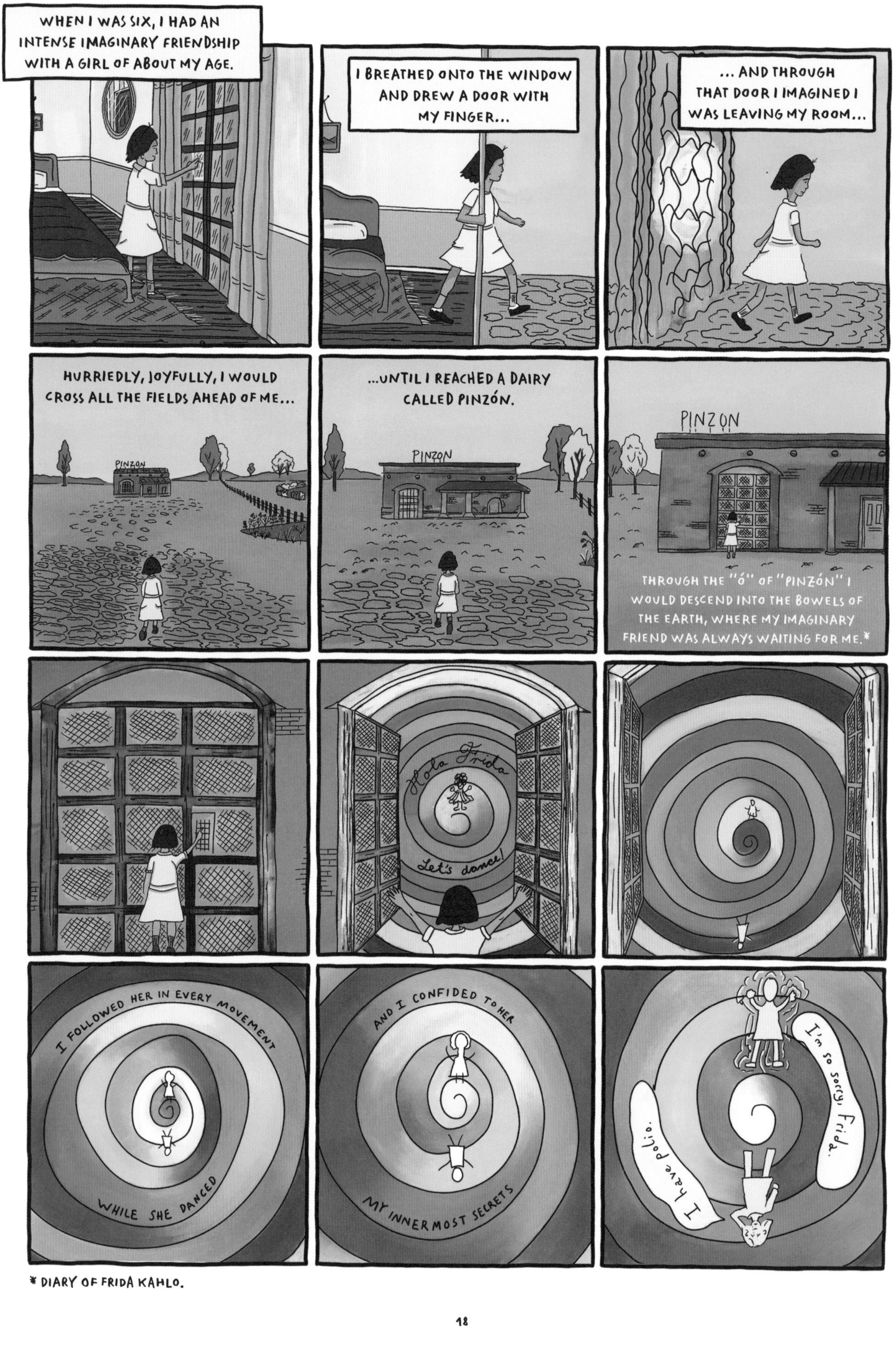

WHEN I WAS SIX, I HAD AN INTENSE IMAGINARY FRIENDSHIP WITH A GIRL OF ABOUT MY AGE.
I BREATHED ONTO THE WINDOW AND DREW A DOOR WITH MY FINGER...
... AND THROUGH THAT DOOR I IMAGINED I WAS LEAVING MY ROOM...
HURRIEDLY, JOYFULLY, I WOULD CROSS ALL THE FIELDS AHEAD OF ME...
PINZON
...UNTIL I REACHED A DAIRY CALLED PINZÓN.
PINZON
PINZON
THROUGH THE "Ó" OF "PINZÓN" I WOULD DESCEND INTO THE BOWELS OF THE EARTH, WHERE MY IMAGINARY FRIEND WAS ALWAYS WAITING FOR ME.*
Hola Frida
Let's dance!
I FOLLOWED HER IN EVERY MOVEMENT
WHILE SHE DANCED
AND I CONFIDED TO HER
MY INNERMOST SECRETS
I'm so sorry, Frida.
I have polio.


* DIARY OF FRIDA KAHLO.

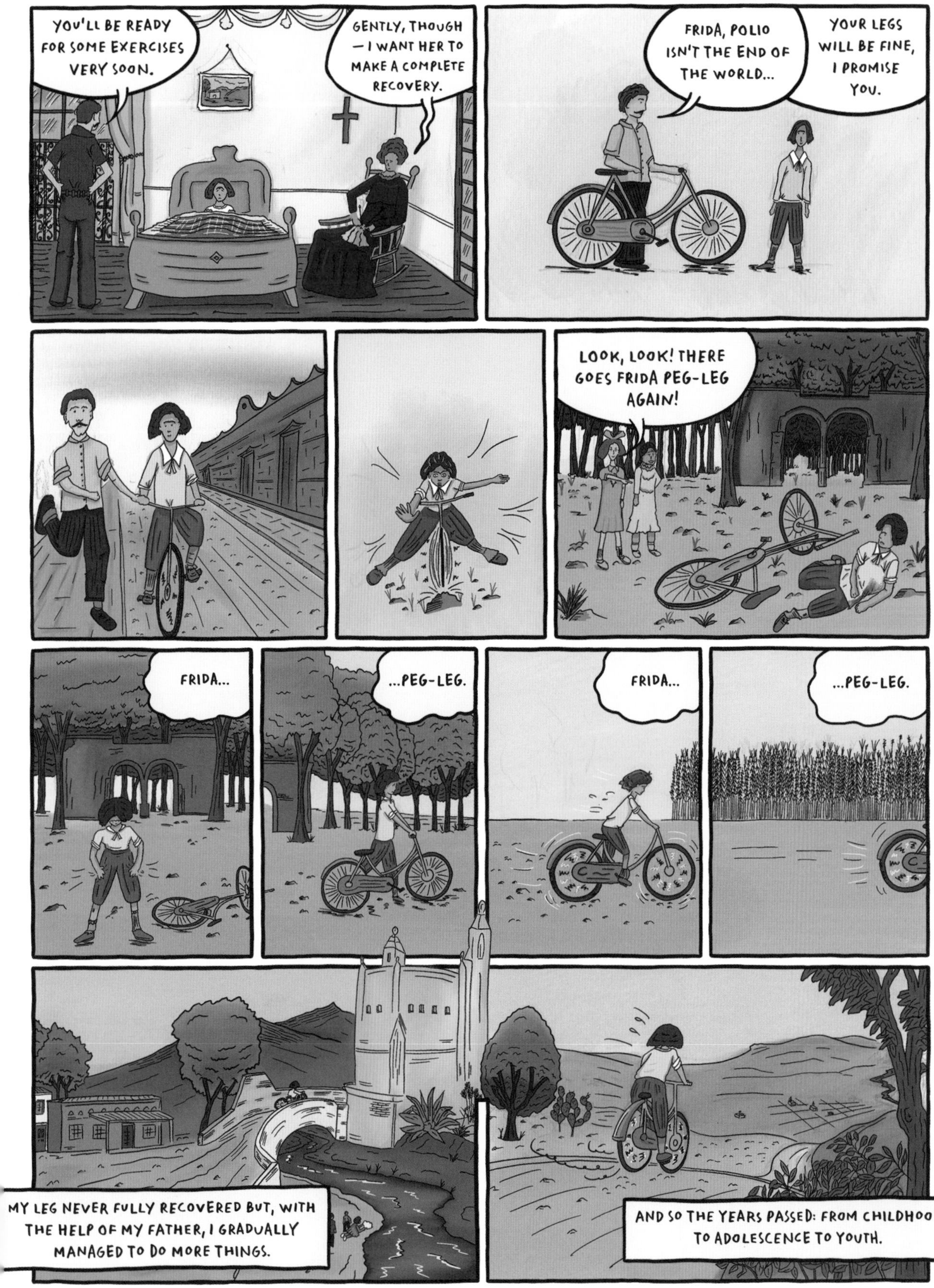
YOU'LL BE READY FOR SOME EXERCISES VERY SOON.
GENTLY, THOUGH — I WANT HER TO MAKE A COMPLETE RECOVERY.
FRIDA, POLIO ISN'T THE END OF THE WORLD...
YOUR LEGS WILL BE FINE, I PROMISE YOU.
LOOK, LOOK! THERE GOES FRIDA PEG-LEG AGAIN!
FRIDA...
...PEG-LEG.
FRIDA...
...PEG-LEG.
MY LEG NEVER FULLY RECOVERED BUT, WITH THE HELP OF MY FATHER, I GRADUALLY MANAGED TO DO MORE THINGS.
AND SO THE YEARS PASSED: FROM CHILDHOOD TO ADOLESCENCE TO YOUTH.

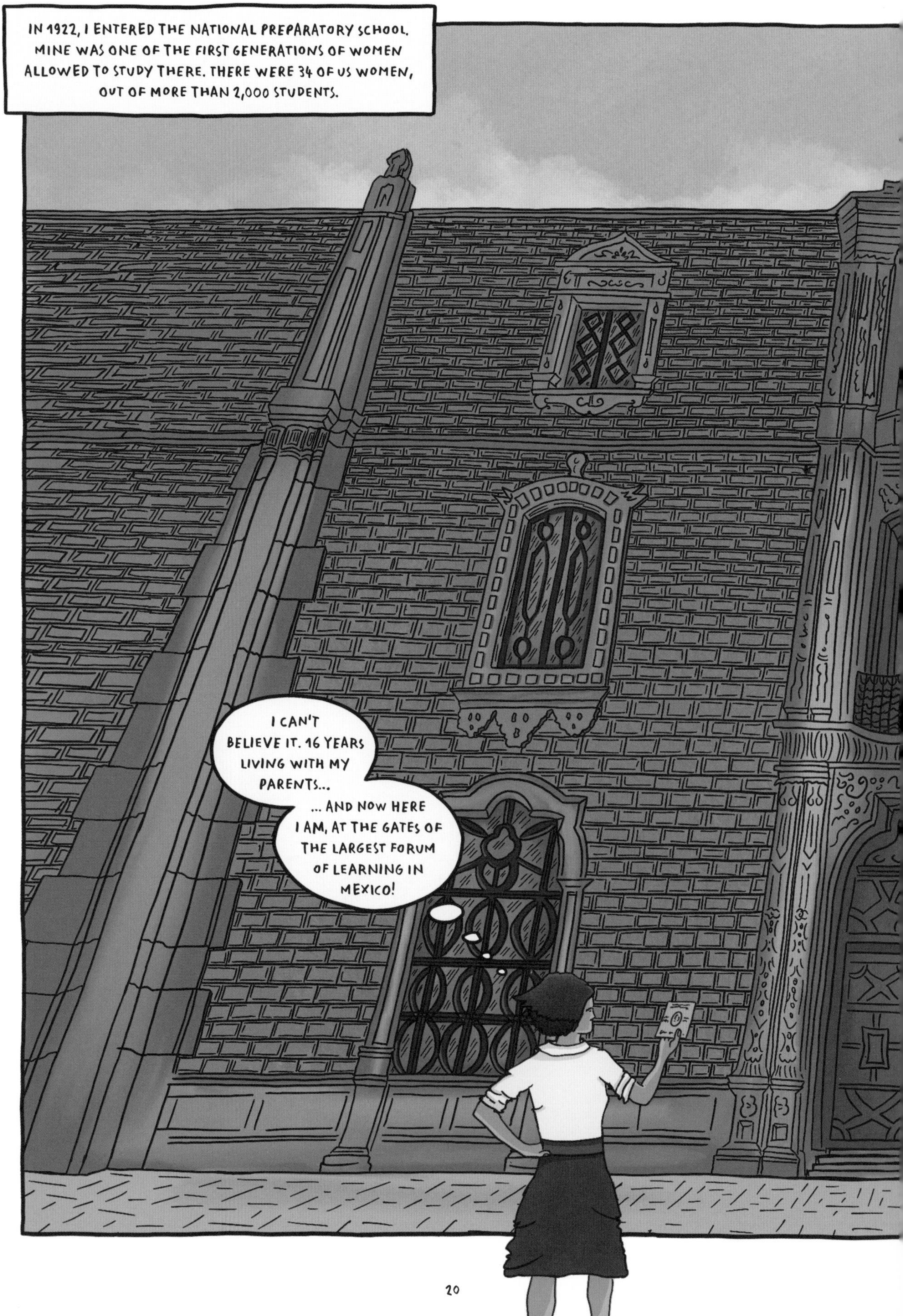
IN 1922, I ENTERED THE NATIONAL PREPARATORY SCHOOL. MINE WAS ONE OF THE FIRST GENERATIONS OF WOMEN ALLOWED TO STUDY THERE. THERE WERE 34 OF US WOMEN, OUT OF MORE THAN 2,000 STUDENTS.
I CAN'T BELIEVE IT. 16 YEARS LIVING WITH MY PARENTS...
... AND NOW HERE I AM, AT THE GATES OF THE LARGEST FORUM OF LEARNING IN MEXICO!

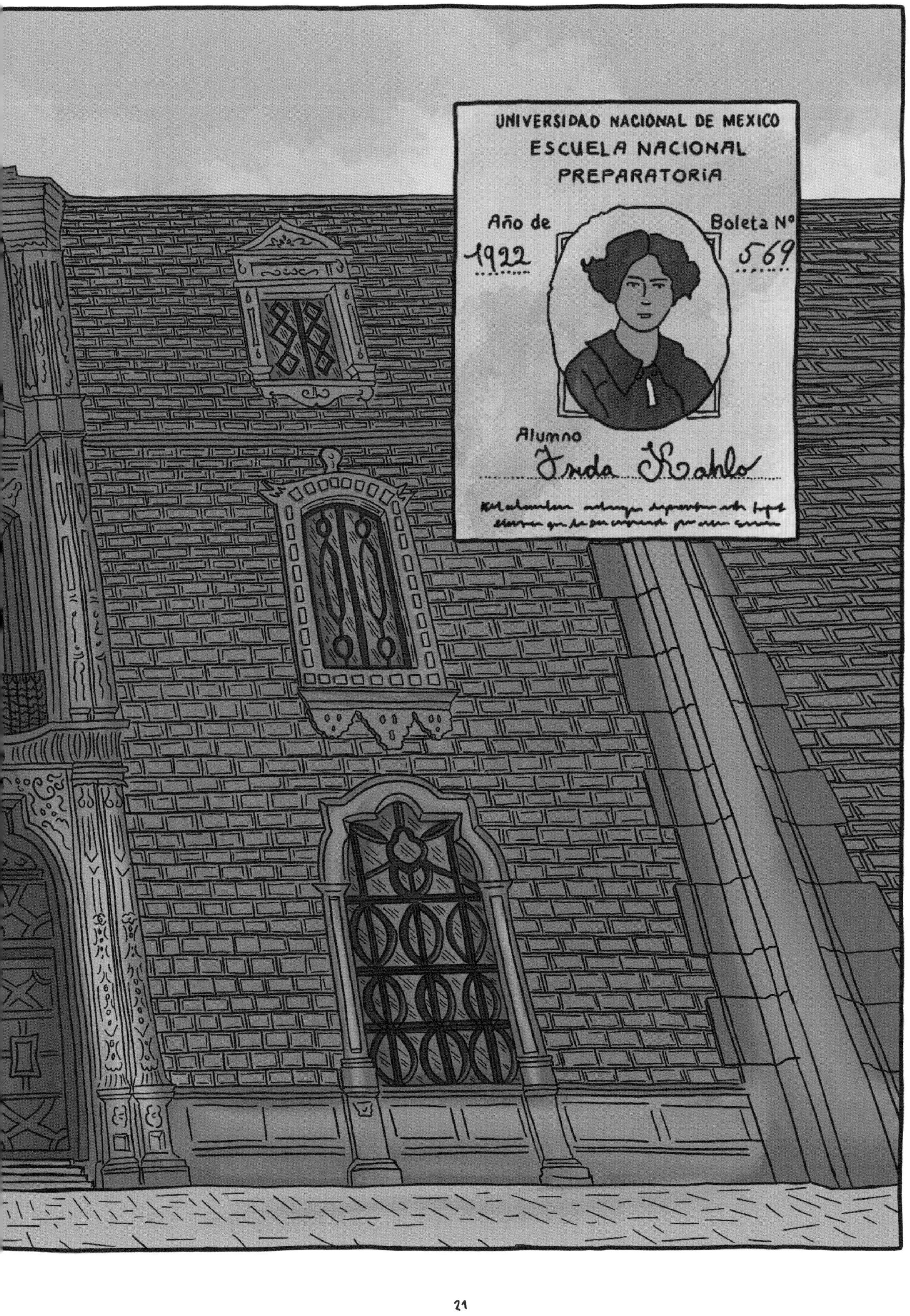
UNIVERSIDAD NACIONAL DE MEXICO
ESCUELA NACIONAL
PREPARATORIA
Año de
1922
Boleta Nº
569
Alumno
Frida Kahlo

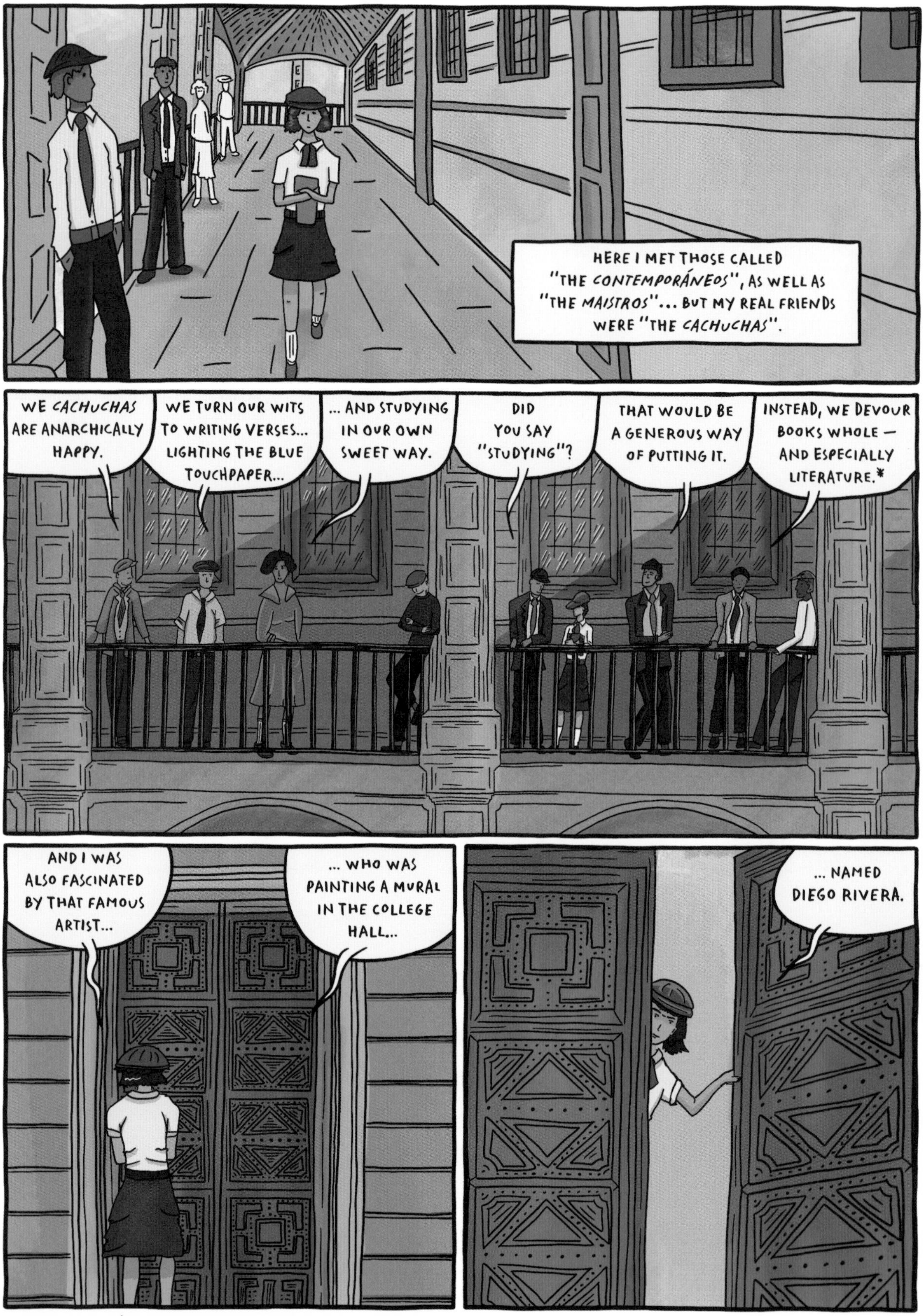
HERE I MET THOSE CALLED "THE *CONTEMPORÁNEOS*", AS WELL AS "THE *MAISTROS*"... BUT MY REAL FRIENDS WERE "THE *CACHUCHAS*".
WE *CACHUCHAS* ARE ANARCHICALLY HAPPY.
WE TURN OUR WITS TO WRITING VERSES... LIGHTING THE BLUE TOUCHPAPER...
... AND STUDYING IN OUR OWN SWEET WAY.
DID YOU SAY "STUDYING"?
THAT WOULD BE A GENEROUS WAY OF PUTTING IT.
INSTEAD, WE DEVOUR BOOKS WHOLE — AND ESPECIALLY LITERATURE.*
AND I WAS ALSO FASCINATED BY THAT FAMOUS ARTIST...
... WHO WAS PAINTING A MURAL IN THE COLLEGE HALL...
... NAMED DIEGO RIVERA.

* MANUEL GONZÁLEZ RAMÍREZ (MEMBER OF THE "CACHUCHAS").

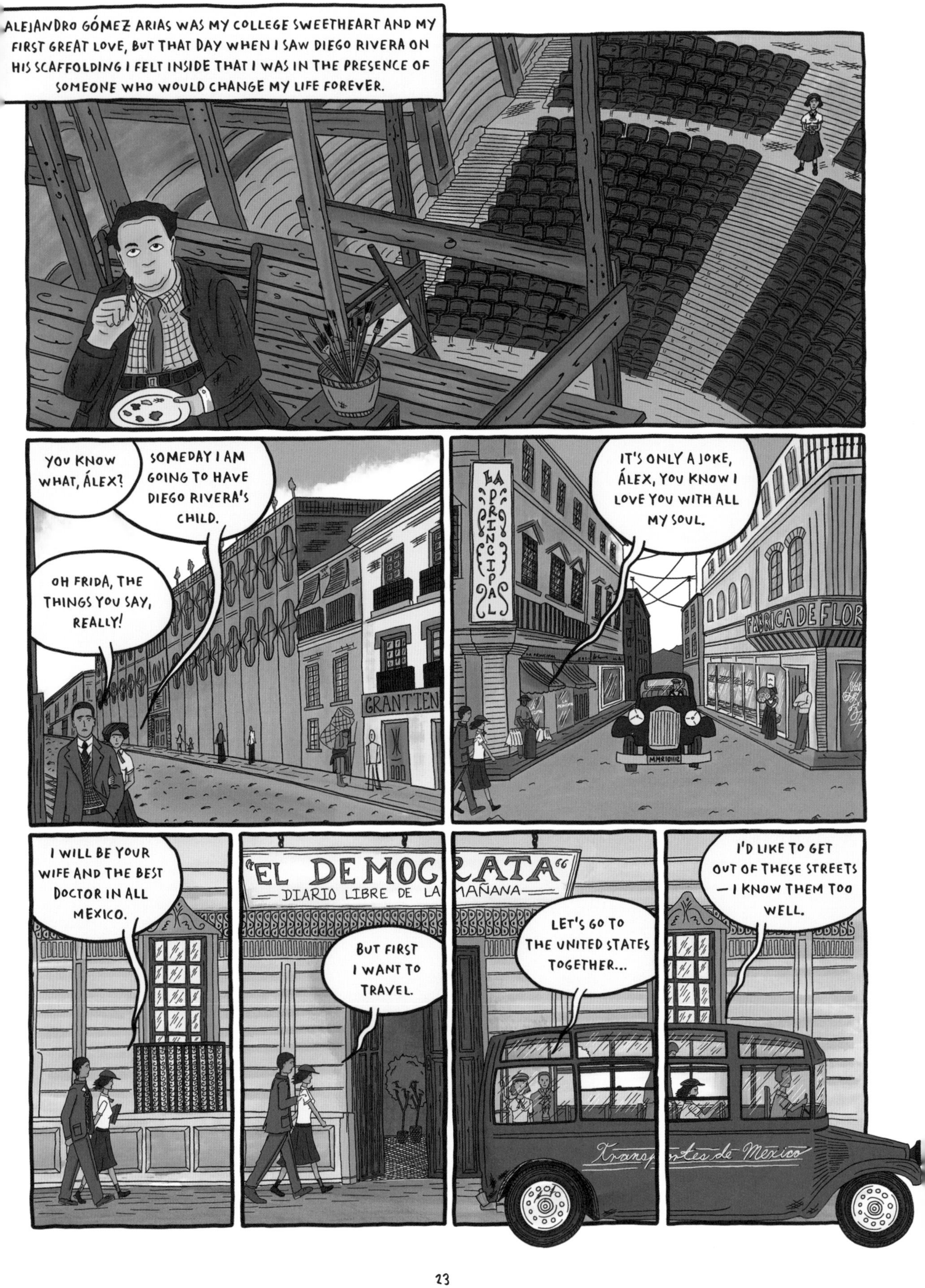
ALEJANDRO GÓMEZ ARIAS WAS MY COLLEGE SWEETHEART AND MY FIRST GREAT LOVE, BUT THAT DAY WHEN I SAW DIEGO RIVERA ON HIS SCAFFOLDING I FELT INSIDE THAT I WAS IN THE PRESENCE OF SOMEONE WHO WOULD CHANGE MY LIFE FOREVER.
YOU KNOW WHAT, ÁLEX?
SOMEDAY I AM GOING TO HAVE DIEGO RIVERA'S CHILD.
OH FRIDA, THE THINGS YOU SAY, REALLY!
GRANTIEN
LA PRINCIPAL
IT'S ONLY A JOKE, ÁLEX, YOU KNOW I LOVE YOU WITH ALL MY SOUL.
FABRICA DE FLOR
MMR10112
I WILL BE YOUR WIFE AND THE BEST DOCTOR IN ALL MEXICO.
"EL DEMOCRATA"
DIARIO LIBRE DE LA MAÑANA
BUT FIRST I WANT TO TRAVEL.
LET'S GO TO THE UNITED STATES TOGETHER...
I'D LIKE TO GET OUT OF THESE STREETS — I KNOW THEM TOO WELL.
Transportes de Mexico

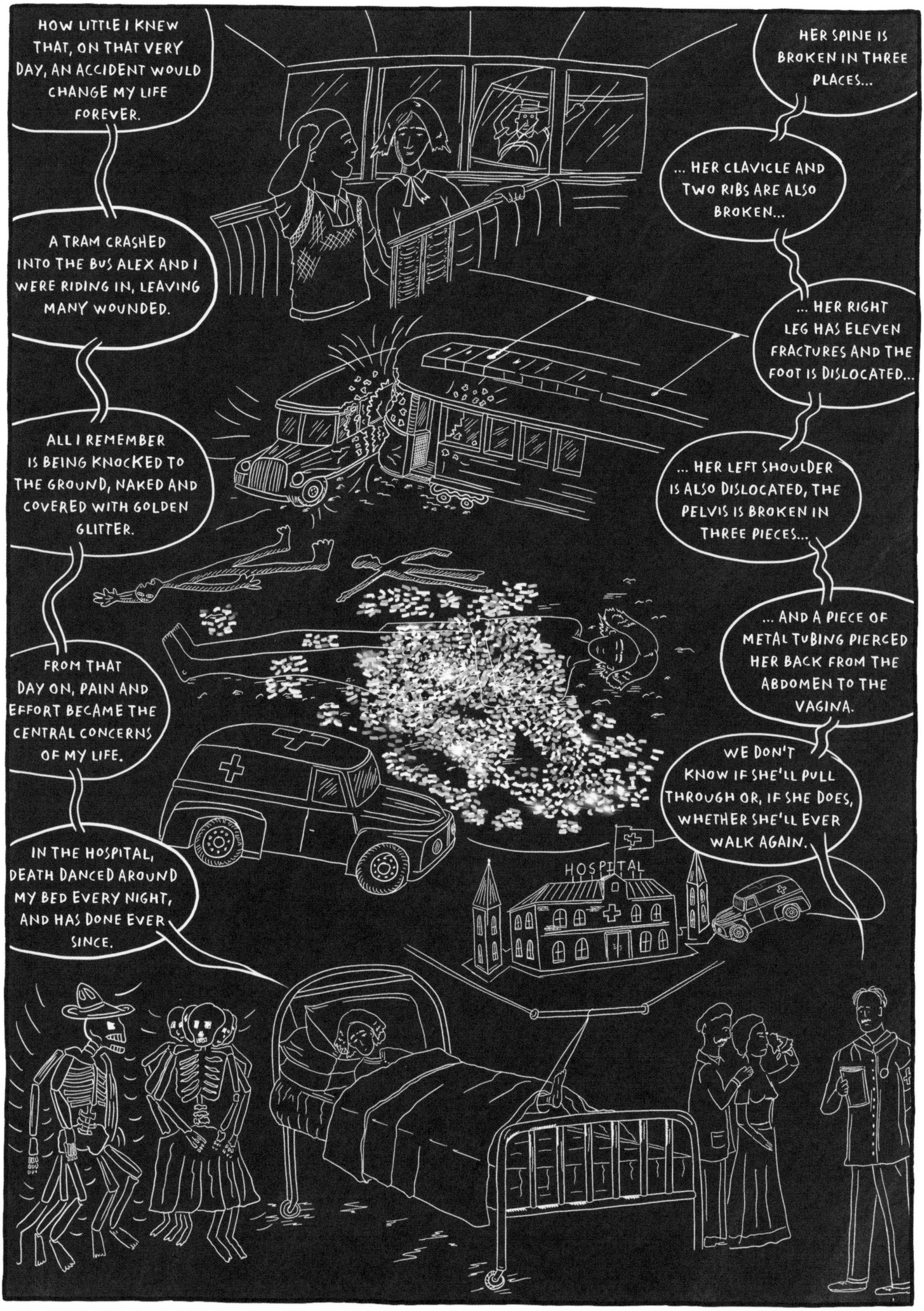
HOW LITTLE I KNEW THAT, ON THAT VERY DAY, AN ACCIDENT WOULD CHANGE MY LIFE FOREVER.
A TRAM CRASHED INTO THE BUS ALEX AND I WERE RIDING IN, LEAVING MANY WOUNDED.
ALL I REMEMBER IS BEING KNOCKED TO THE GROUND, NAKED AND COVERED WITH GOLDEN GLITTER.
FROM THAT DAY ON, PAIN AND EFFORT BECAME THE CENTRAL CONCERNS OF MY LIFE.
IN THE HOSPITAL, DEATH DANCED AROUND MY BED EVERY NIGHT, AND HAS DONE EVER SINCE.
HER SPINE IS BROKEN IN THREE PLACES...
... HER CLAVICLE AND TWO RIBS ARE ALSO BROKEN...
... HER RIGHT LEG HAS ELEVEN FRACTURES AND THE FOOT IS DISLOCATED...
... HER LEFT SHOULDER IS ALSO DISLOCATED, THE PELVIS IS BROKEN IN THREE PIECES...
... AND A PIECE OF METAL TUBING PIERCED HER BACK FROM THE ABDOMEN TO THE VAGINA.
WE DON'T KNOW IF SHE'LL PULL THROUGH OR, IF SHE DOES, WHETHER SHE'LL EVER WALK AGAIN.
HOSPITAL

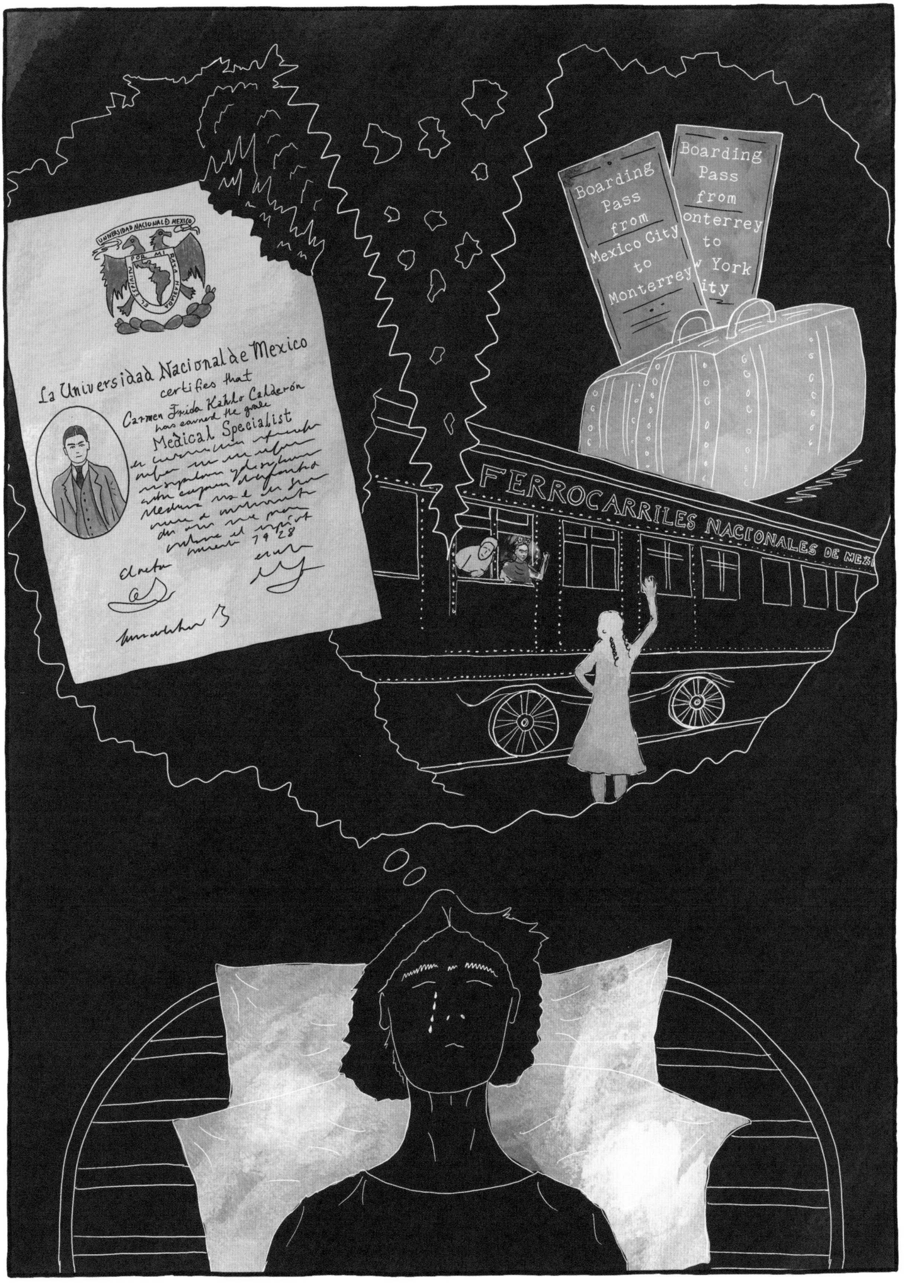
UNIVERSIDAD NACIONAL DE MEXICO
POR MI RAZA HABLARA EL ESPIRITU
La Universidad Nacional de Mexico
certifies that
Carmen Frida Kahlo Calderón
has earned the grade
Medical Specialist
1928
Boarding Pass from Mexico City to Monterrey
Boarding Pass from
FERROCARRILES NACIONALES

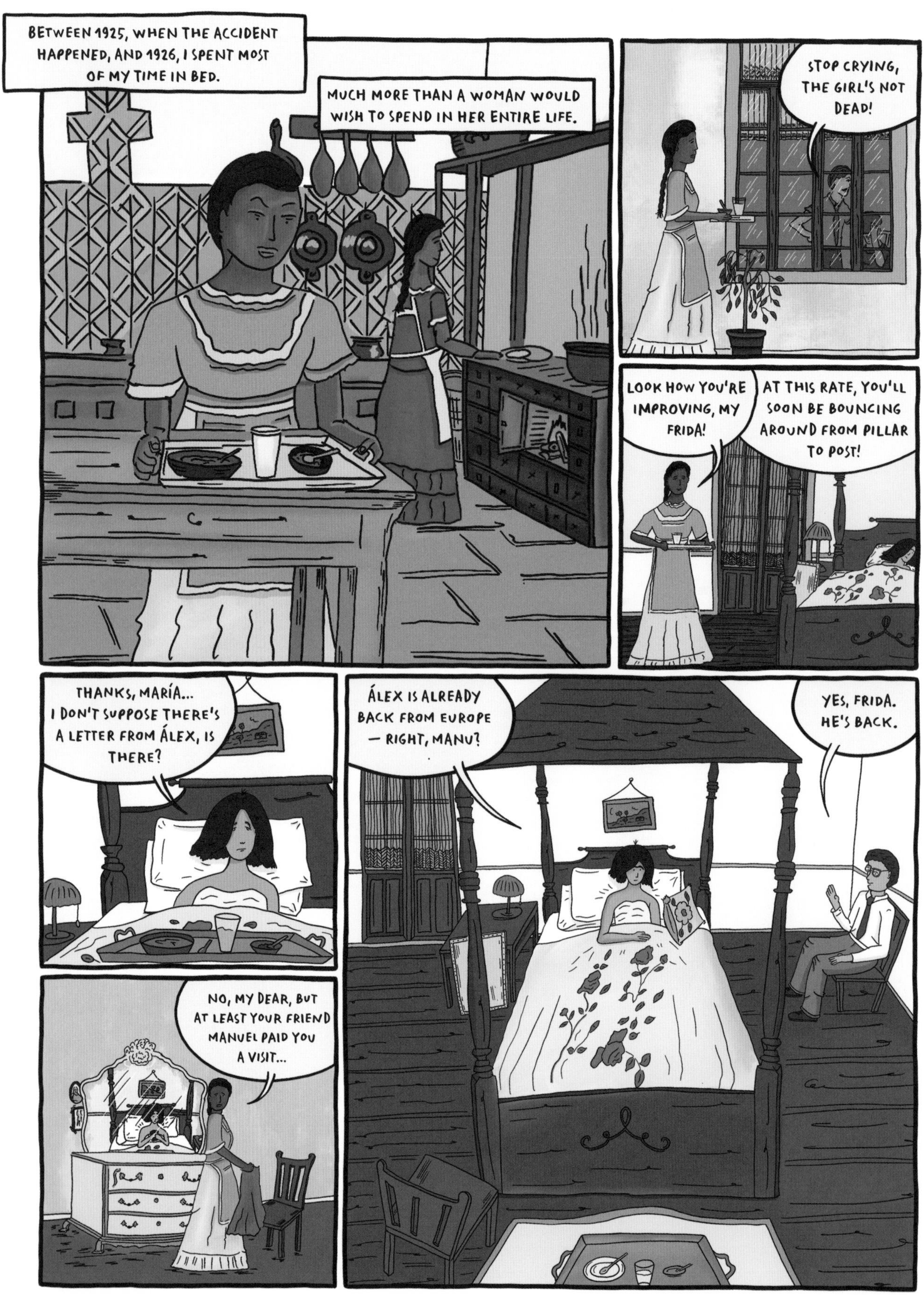
BETWEEN 1925, WHEN THE ACCIDENT HAPPENED, AND 1926, I SPENT MOST OF MY TIME IN BED.
MUCH MORE THAN A WOMAN WOULD WISH TO SPEND IN HER ENTIRE LIFE.
STOP CRYING, THE GIRL'S NOT DEAD!
LOOK HOW YOU'RE IMPROVING, MY FRIDA!
AT THIS RATE, YOU'LL SOON BE BOUNCING AROUND FROM PILLAR TO POST!
THANKS, MARÍA... I DON'T SUPPOSE THERE'S A LETTER FROM ÁLEX, IS THERE?
NO, MY DEAR, BUT AT LEAST YOUR FRIEND MANUEL PAID YOU A VISIT...
ÁLEX IS ALREADY BACK FROM EUROPE — RIGHT, MANU?
YES, FRIDA. HE'S BACK.

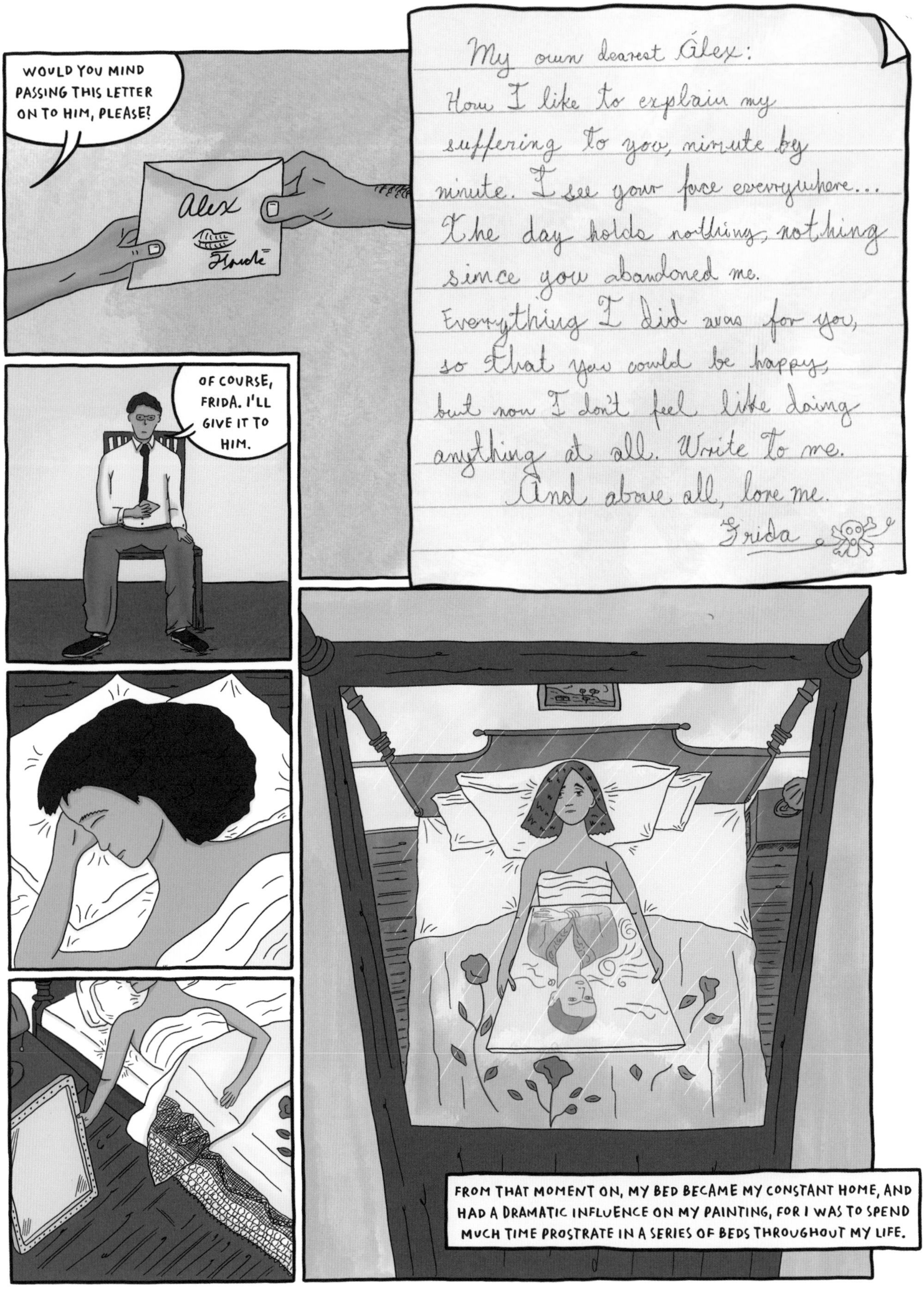

WOULD YOU MIND PASSING THIS LETTER ON TO HIM, PLEASE?
Alex
Frida
My own dearest Álex:
How I like to explain my suffering to you, minute by minute. I see your face everywhere... The day holds nothing, nothing since you abandoned me.
Everything I did was for you, so that you could be happy, but now I don't feel like doing anything at all. Write to me.
And above all, love me.
Frida
OF COURSE, FRIDA. I'LL GIVE IT TO HIM.
FROM THAT MOMENT ON, MY BED BECAME MY CONSTANT HOME, AND HAD A DRAMATIC INFLUENCE ON MY PAINTING, FOR I WAS TO SPEND MUCH TIME PROSTRATE IN A SERIES OF BEDS THROUGHOUT MY LIFE.

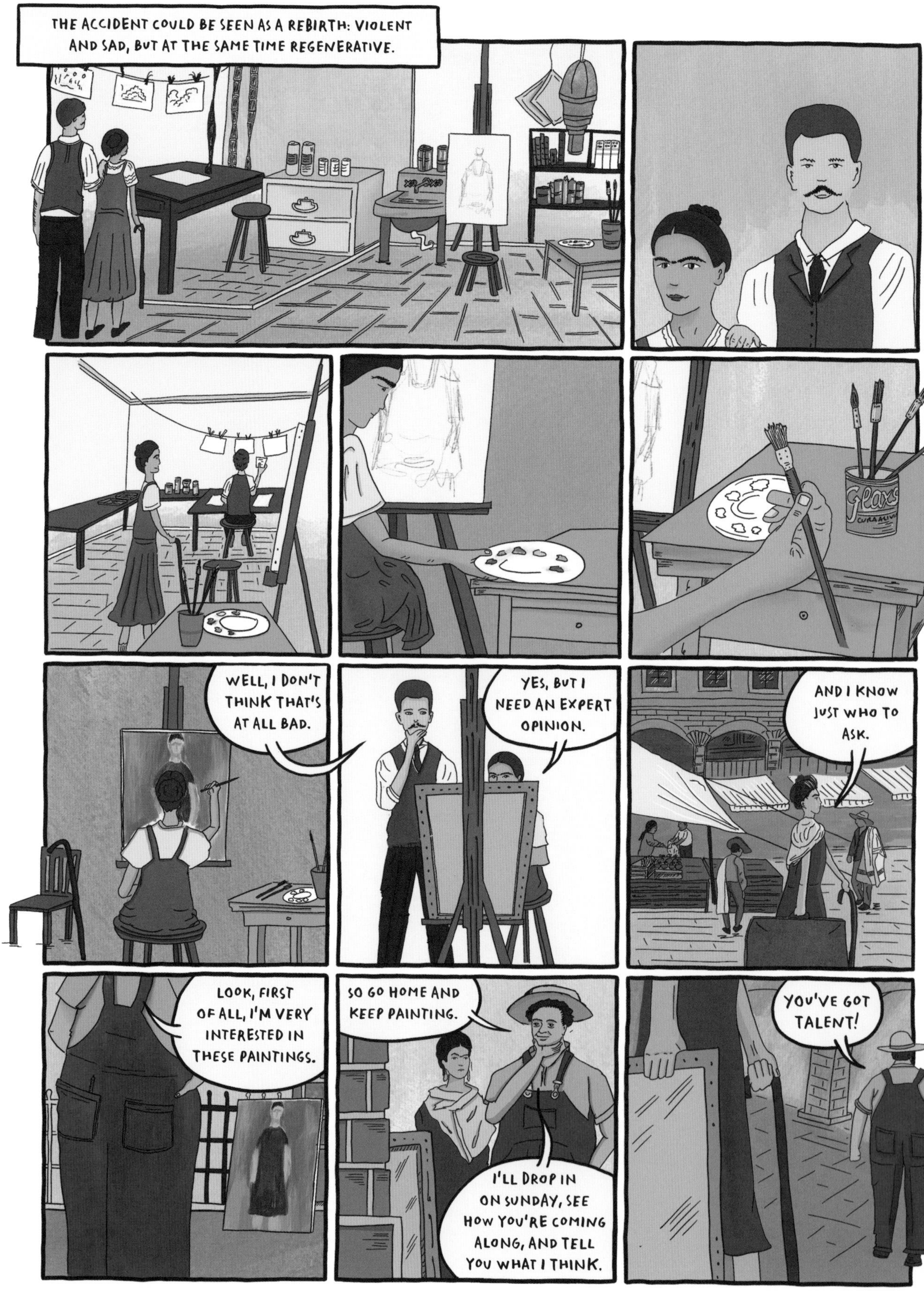
THE ACCIDENT COULD BE SEEN AS A REBIRTH: VIOLENT AND SAD, BUT AT THE SAME TIME REGENERATIVE.
WELL, I DON'T THINK THAT'S AT ALL BAD.
YES, BUT I NEED AN EXPERT OPINION.
AND I KNOW JUST WHO TO ASK.
LOOK, FIRST OF ALL, I'M VERY INTERESTED IN THESE PAINTINGS.
SO GO HOME AND KEEP PAINTING.
I'LL DROP IN ON SUNDAY, SEE HOW YOU'RE COMING ALONG, AND TELL YOU WHAT I THINK.
YOU'VE GOT TALENT!

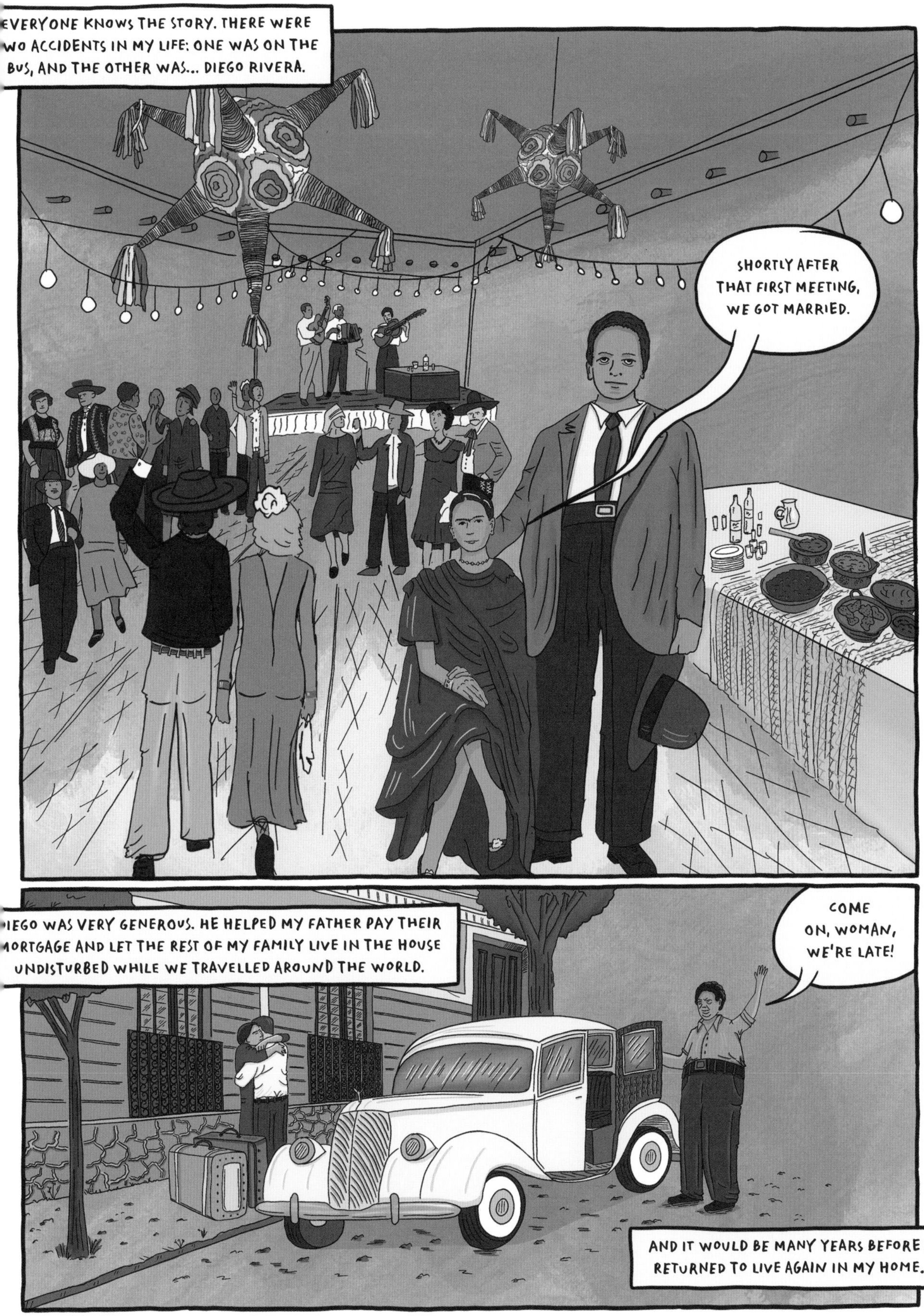
EVERYONE KNOWS THE STORY. THERE WERE
WO ACCIDENTS IN MY LIFE: ONE WAS ON THE
BUS, AND THE OTHER WAS... DIEGO RIVERA.
SHORTLY AFTER THAT FIRST MEETING, WE GOT MARRIED.
IEGO WAS VERY GENEROUS. HE HELPED MY FATHER PAY THEIR
ORTGAGE AND LET THE REST OF MY FAMILY LIVE IN THE HOUSE
UNDISTURBED WHILE WE TRAVELLED AROUND THE WORLD.
COME ON, WOMAN, WE'RE LATE!
AND IT WOULD BE MANY YEARS BEFORE I RETURNED TO LIVE AGAIN IN MY HOME.

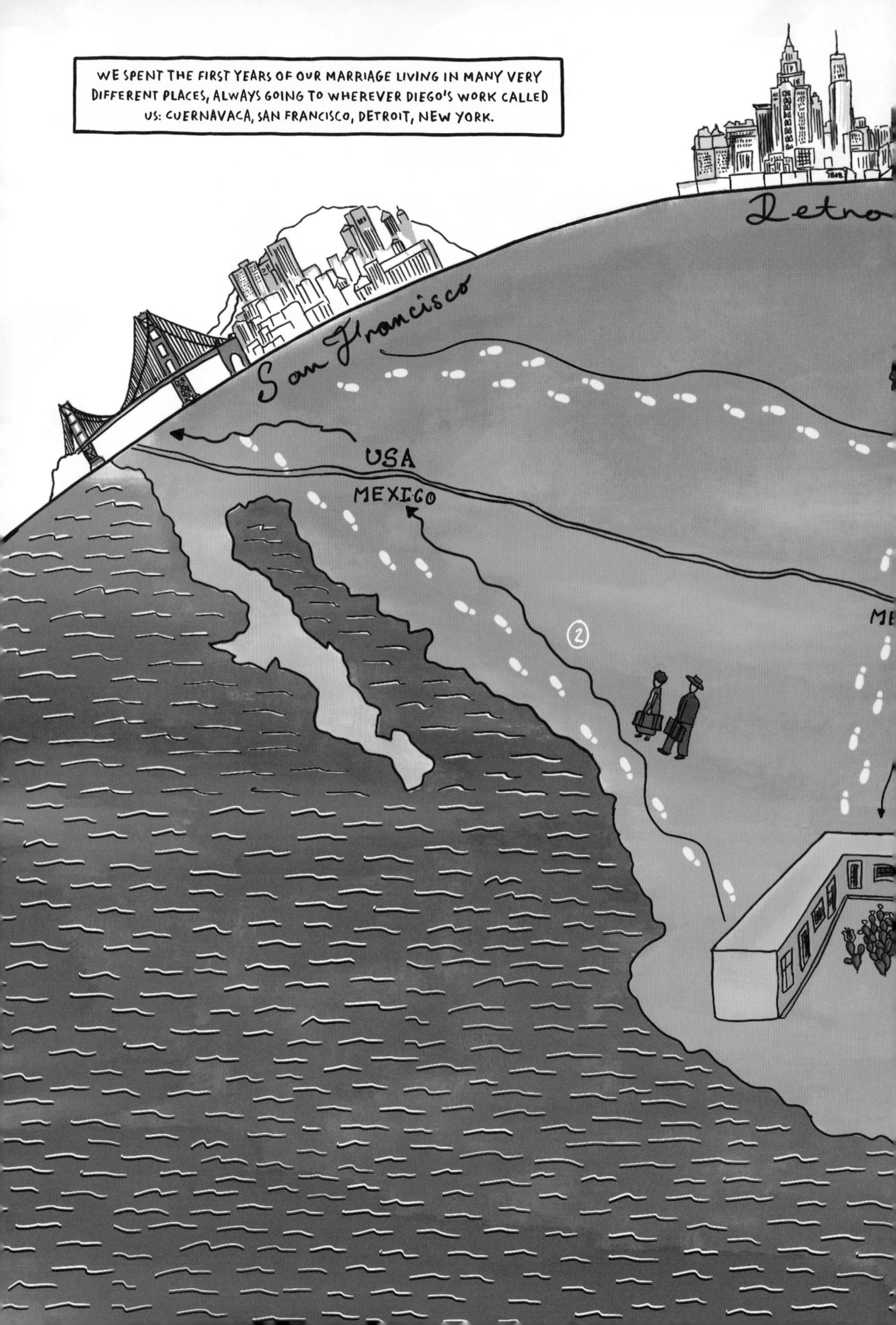
WE SPENT THE FIRST YEARS OF OUR MARRIAGE LIVING IN MANY VERY DIFFERENT PLACES, ALWAYS GOING TO WHEREVER DIEGO'S WORK CALLED US: CUERNAVACA, SAN FRANCISCO, DETROIT, NEW YORK.
San Francisco
USA
MEXICO
2

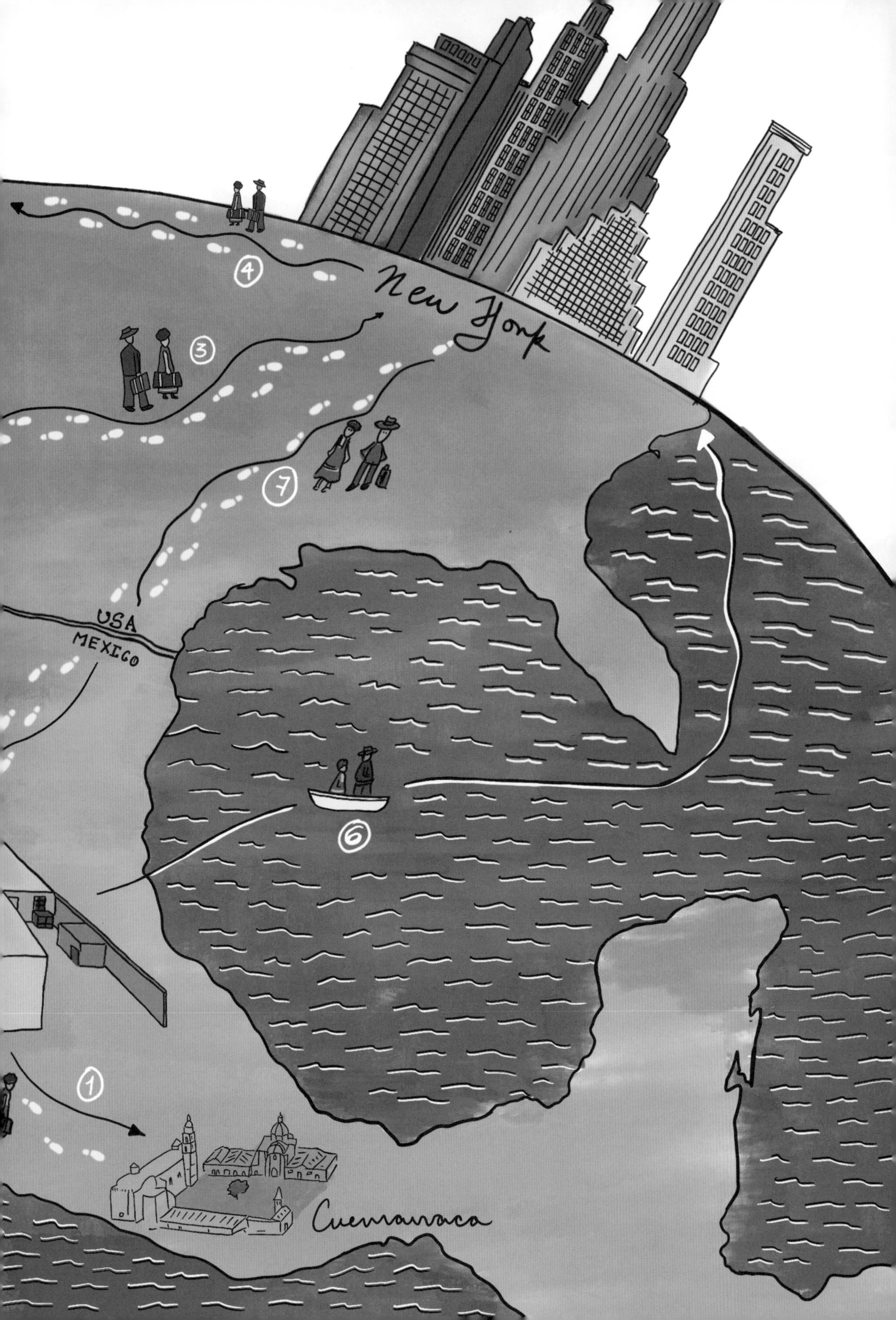
New York
4
3
7
USA
MEXICO
6
1
Cuernavaca

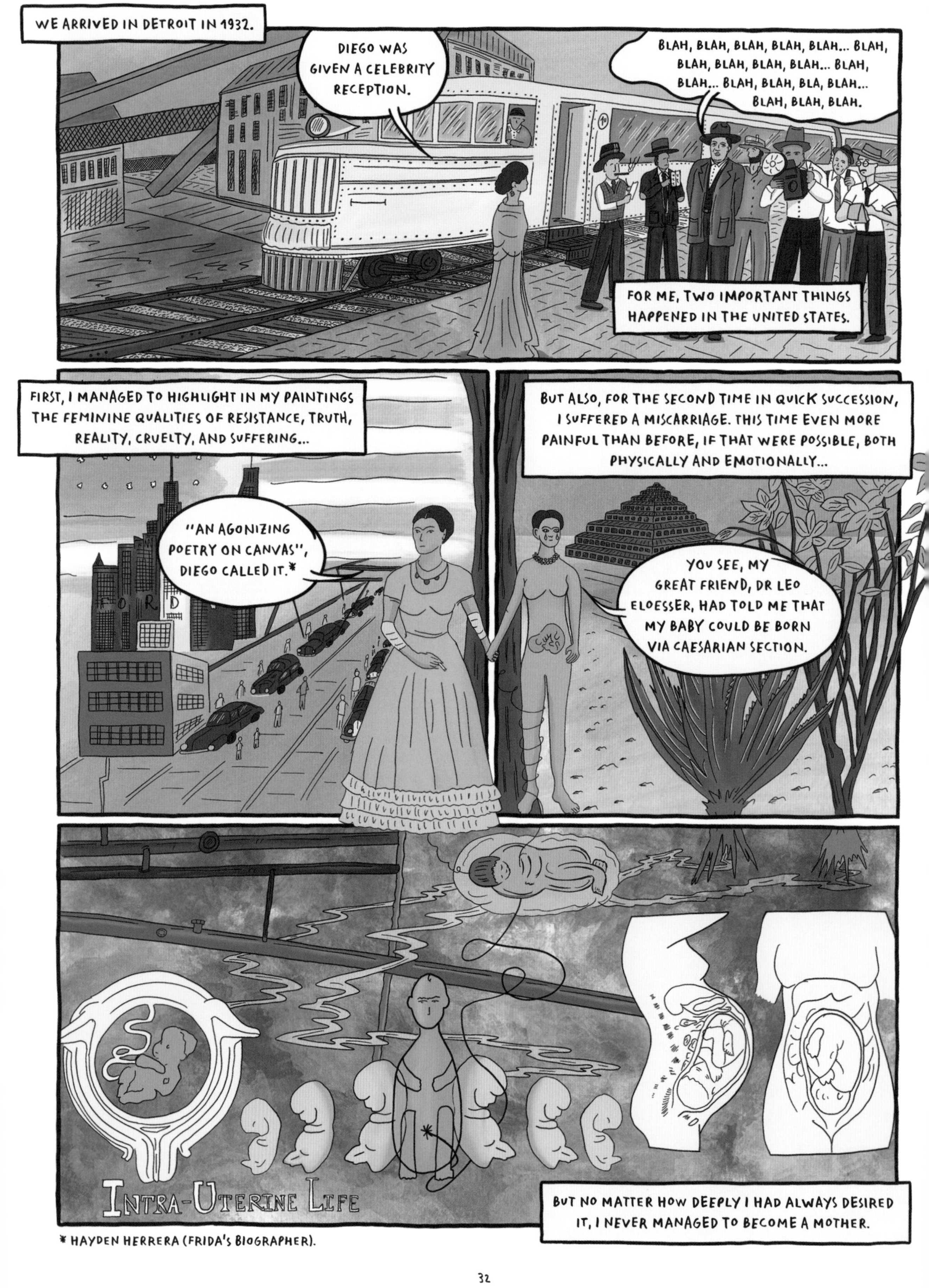
WE ARRIVED IN DETROIT IN 1932.
DIEGO WAS GIVEN A CELEBRITY RECEPTION.
BLAH, BLAH, BLAH, BLAH, BLAH... BLAH, BLAH, BLAH, BLAH, BLAH... BLAH, BLAH... BLAH, BLAH, BLA, BLAH... BLAH, BLAH, BLAH.
FOR ME, TWO IMPORTANT THINGS HAPPENED IN THE UNITED STATES.
FIRST, I MANAGED TO HIGHLIGHT IN MY PAINTINGS THE FEMININE QUALITIES OF RESISTANCE, TRUTH, REALITY, CRUELTY, AND SUFFERING...
"AN AGONIZING POETRY ON CANVAS", DIEGO CALLED IT.*
FORD
BUT ALSO, FOR THE SECOND TIME IN QUICK SUCCESSION, I SUFFERED A MISCARRIAGE. THIS TIME EVEN MORE PAINFUL THAN BEFORE, IF THAT WERE POSSIBLE, BOTH PHYSICALLY AND EMOTIONALLY...
YOU SEE, MY GREAT FRIEND, DR LEO ELOESSER, HAD TOLD ME THAT MY BABY COULD BE BORN VIA CAESARIAN SECTION.
INTRA-UTERINE LIFE
BUT NO MATTER HOW DEEPLY I HAD ALWAYS DESIRED IT, I NEVER MANAGED TO BECOME A MOTHER.

* HAYDEN HERRERA (FRIDA'S BIOGRAPHER).

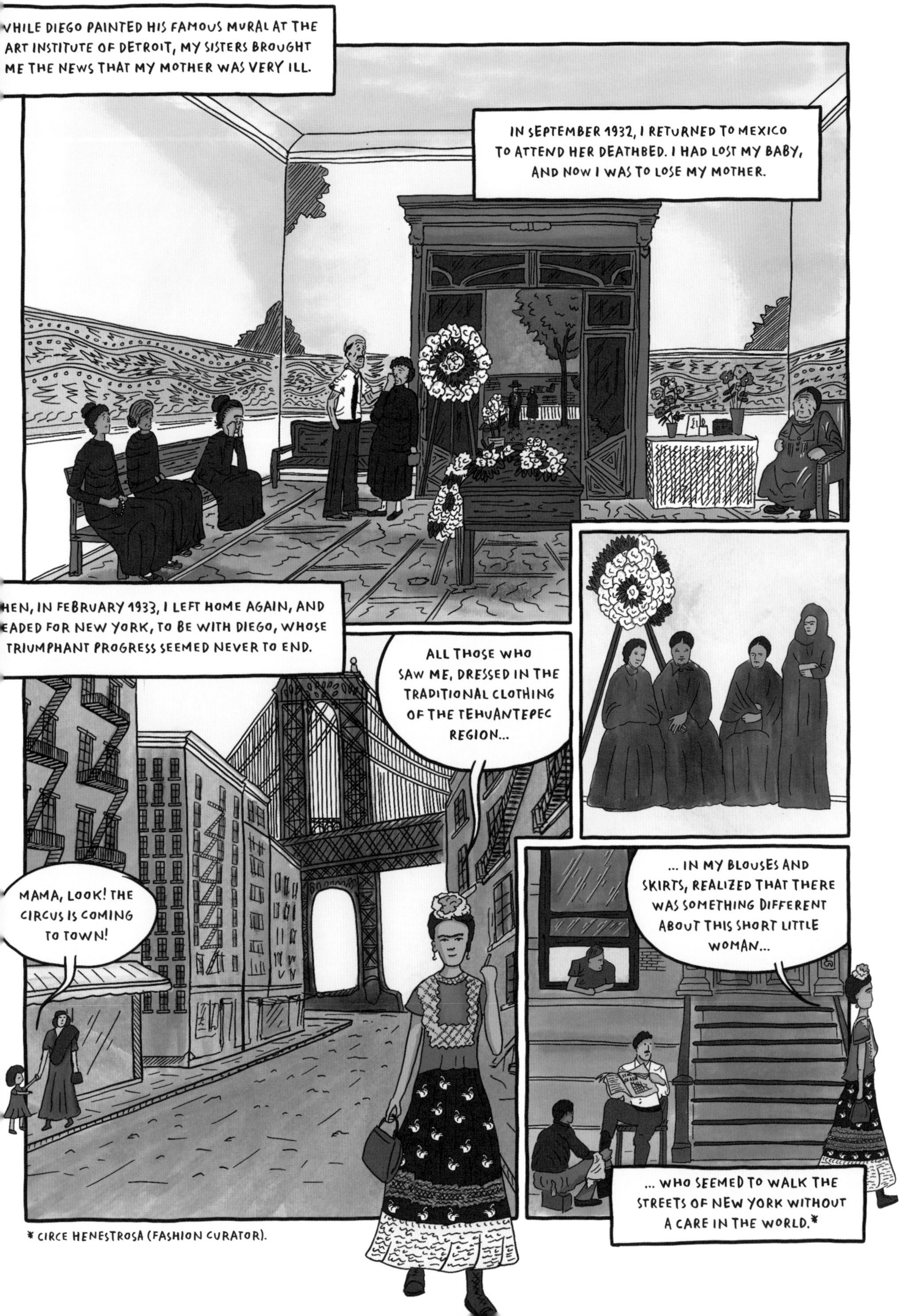
VHILE DIEGO PAINTED HIS FAMOUS MURAL AT THE ART INSTITUTE OF DETROIT, MY SISTERS BROUGHT ME THE NEWS THAT MY MOTHER WAS VERY ILL.
IN SEPTEMBER 1932, I RETURNED TO MEXICO TO ATTEND HER DEATHBED. I HAD LOST MY BABY, AND NOW I WAS TO LOSE MY MOTHER.
HEN, IN FEBRUARY 1933, I LEFT HOME AGAIN, AND EADED FOR NEW YORK, TO BE WITH DIEGO, WHOSE TRIUMPHANT PROGRESS SEEMED NEVER TO END.
ALL THOSE WHO SAW ME, DRESSED IN THE TRADITIONAL CLOTHING OF THE TEHUANTEPEC REGION...
MAMA, LOOK! THE CIRCUS IS COMING TO TOWN!
... IN MY BLOUSES AND SKIRTS, REALIZED THAT THERE WAS SOMETHING DIFFERENT ABOUT THIS SHORT LITTLE WOMAN...
... WHO SEEMED TO WALK THE STREETS OF NEW YORK WITHOUT A CARE IN THE WORLD.*

* CIRCE HENESTROSA (FASHION CURATOR).

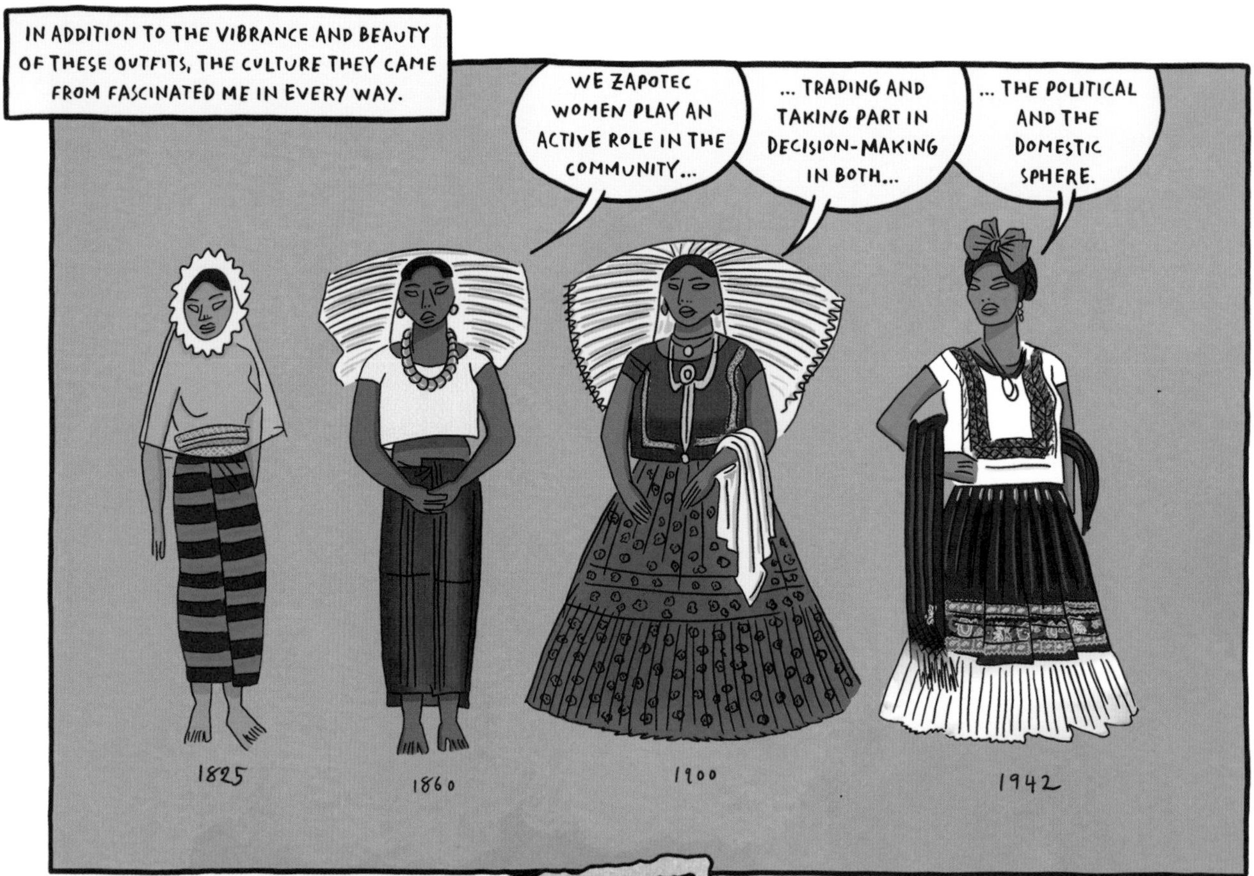
IN ADDITION TO THE VIBRANCE AND BEAUTY OF THESE OUTFITS, THE CULTURE THEY CAME FROM FASCINATED ME IN EVERY WAY.
WE ZAPOTEC WOMEN PLAY AN ACTIVE ROLE IN THE COMMUNITY...
... TRADING AND TAKING PART IN DECISION-MAKING IN BOTH...
... THE POLITICAL AND THE DOMESTIC SPHERE.
1825
1860
1900
1942

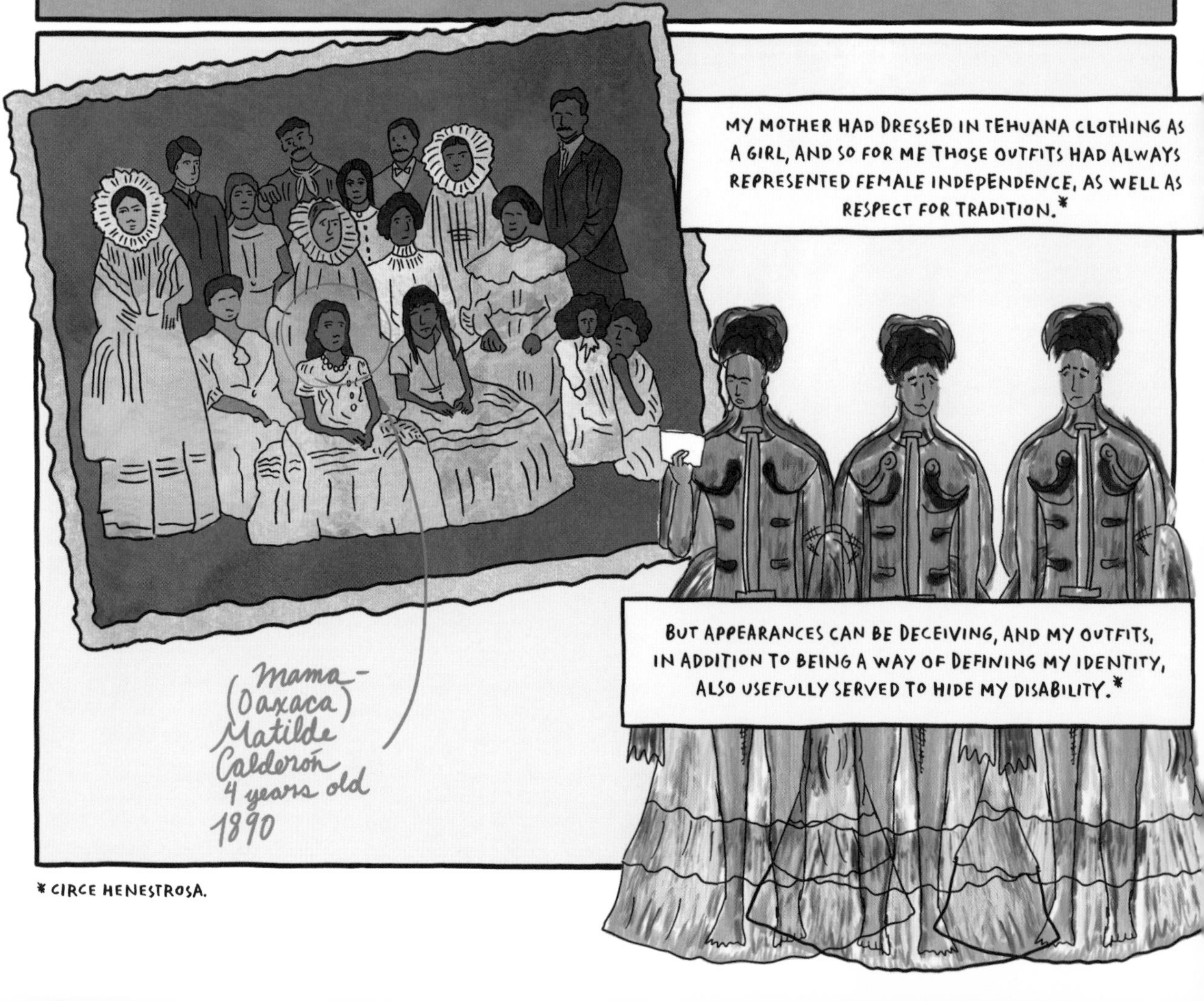
MY MOTHER HAD DRESSED IN TEHUANA CLOTHING AS A GIRL, AND SO FOR ME THOSE OUTFITS HAD ALWAYS REPRESENTED FEMALE INDEPENDENCE, AS WELL AS RESPECT FOR TRADITION.*
Mama- (Oaxaca) Matilde Calderón 4 years old 1890
BUT APPEARANCES CAN BE DECEIVING, AND MY OUTFITS, IN ADDITION TO BEING A WAY OF DEFINING MY IDENTITY, ALSO USEFULLY SERVED TO HIDE MY DISABILITY.*

* CIRCE HENESTROSA.

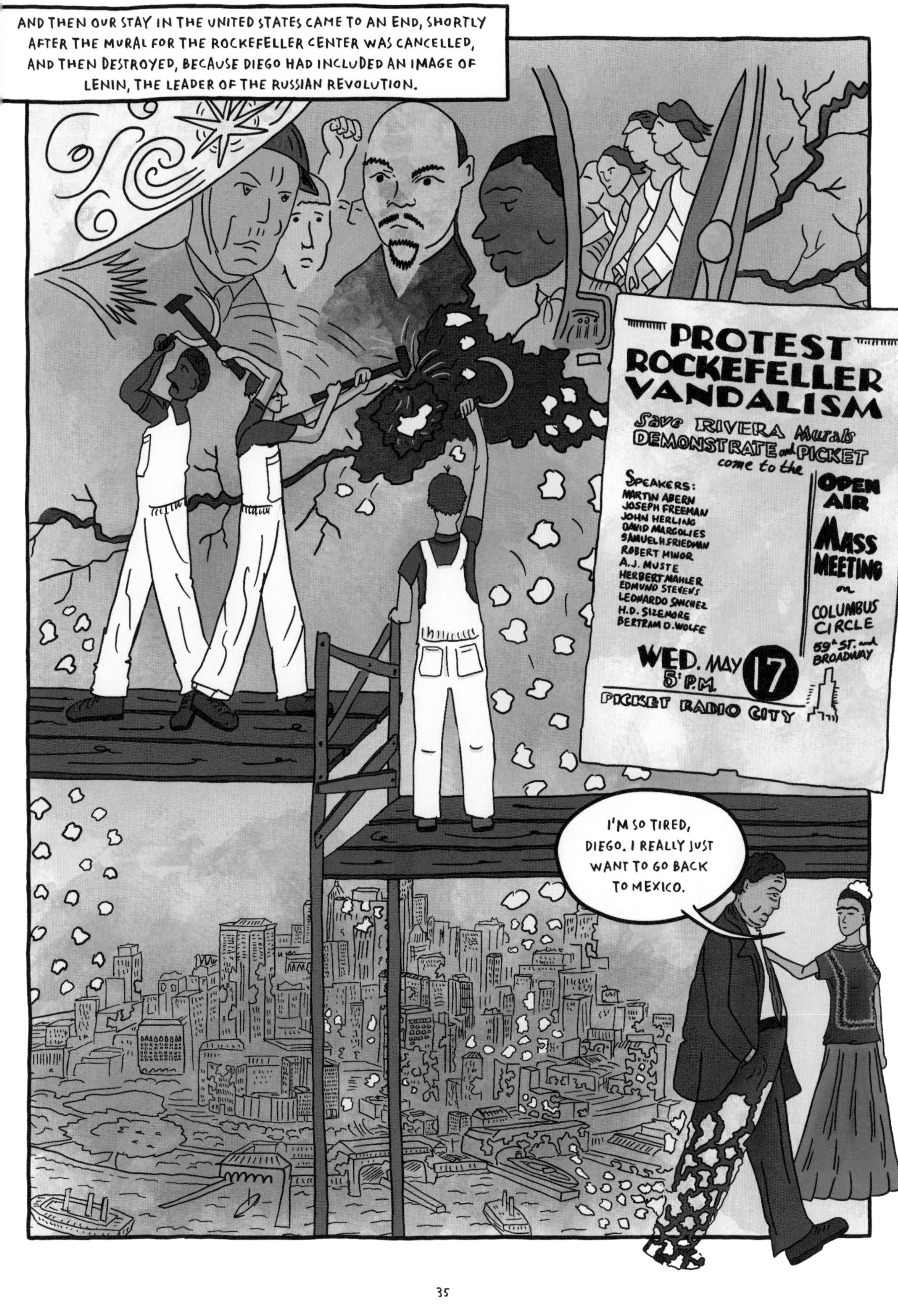
AND THEN OUR STAY IN THE UNITED STATES CAME TO AN END, SHORTLY AFTER THE MURAL FOR THE ROCKEFELLER CENTER WAS CANCELLED, AND THEN DESTROYED, BECAUSE DIEGO HAD INCLUDED AN IMAGE OF LENIN, THE LEADER OF THE RUSSIAN REVOLUTION.
PROTEST ROCKEFELLER VANDALISM
Save RIVERA Murals
DEMONSTRATE and PICKET
come to the
OPEN AIR MASS MEETING on COLUMBUS CIRCLE 59th ST. and BROADWAY
SPEAKERS:
MARTIN ABERN
JOSEPH FREEMAN
JOHN HERLING
DAVID MARGOLIES
SAMUEL H. FRIEDMAN
ROBERT MINOR
A. J. MUSTE
HERBERT MAHLER
EDMUND STEVENS
LEONARDO SANCHEZ
H.D. SIZEMORE
BERTRAM D. WOLFE
WED. MAY 17 5 P.M.
PICKET RADIO CITY
I'M SO TIRED, DIEGO. I REALLY JUST WANT TO GO BACK TO MEXICO.

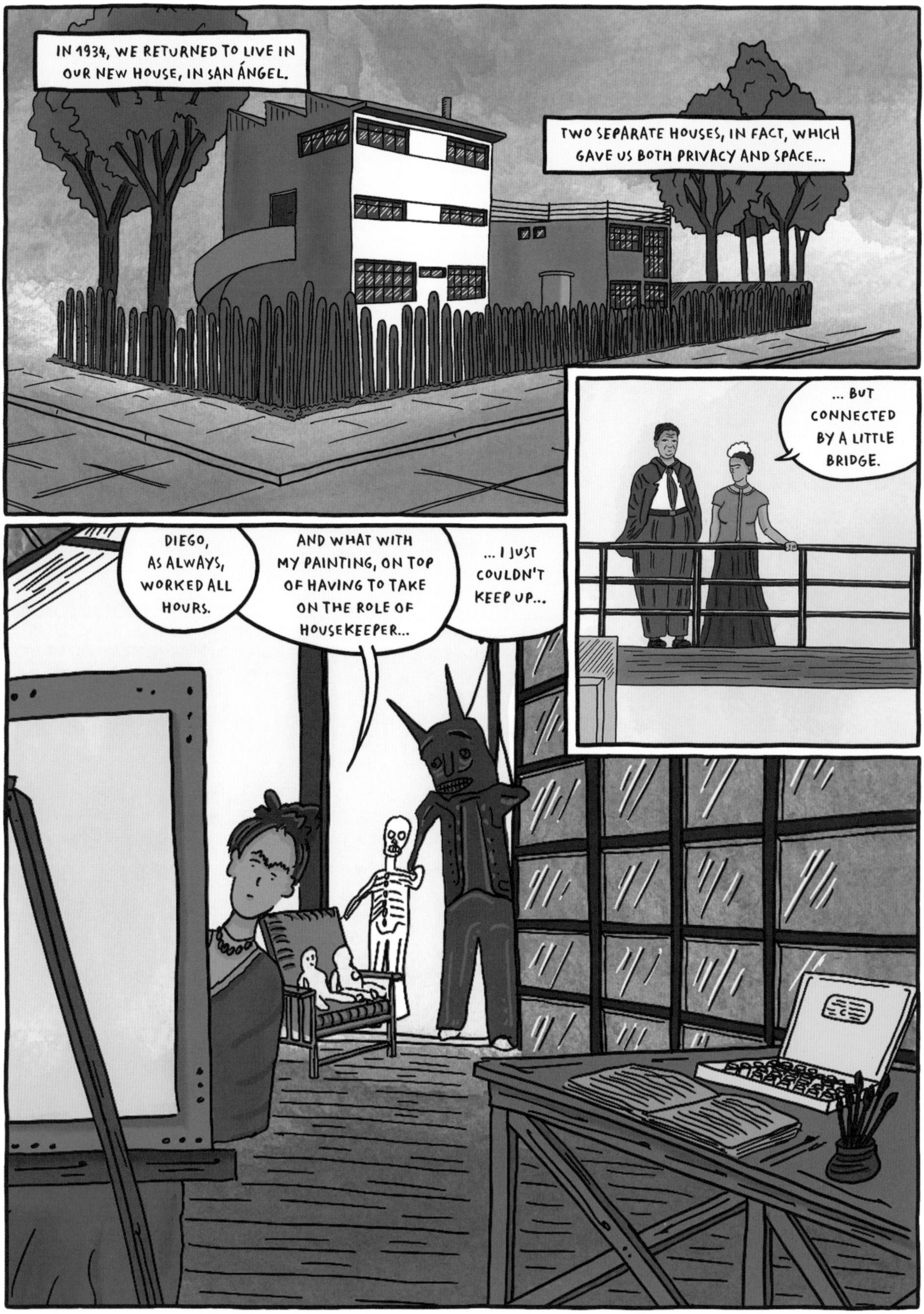
IN 1934, WE RETURNED TO LIVE IN OUR NEW HOUSE, IN SAN ÁNGEL.
TWO SEPARATE HOUSES, IN FACT, WHICH GAVE US BOTH PRIVACY AND SPACE...
... BUT CONNECTED BY A LITTLE BRIDGE.
DIEGO, AS ALWAYS, WORKED ALL HOURS.
AND WHAT WITH MY PAINTING, ON TOP OF HAVING TO TAKE ON THE ROLE OF HOUSEKEEPER...
... I JUST COULDN'T KEEP UP...

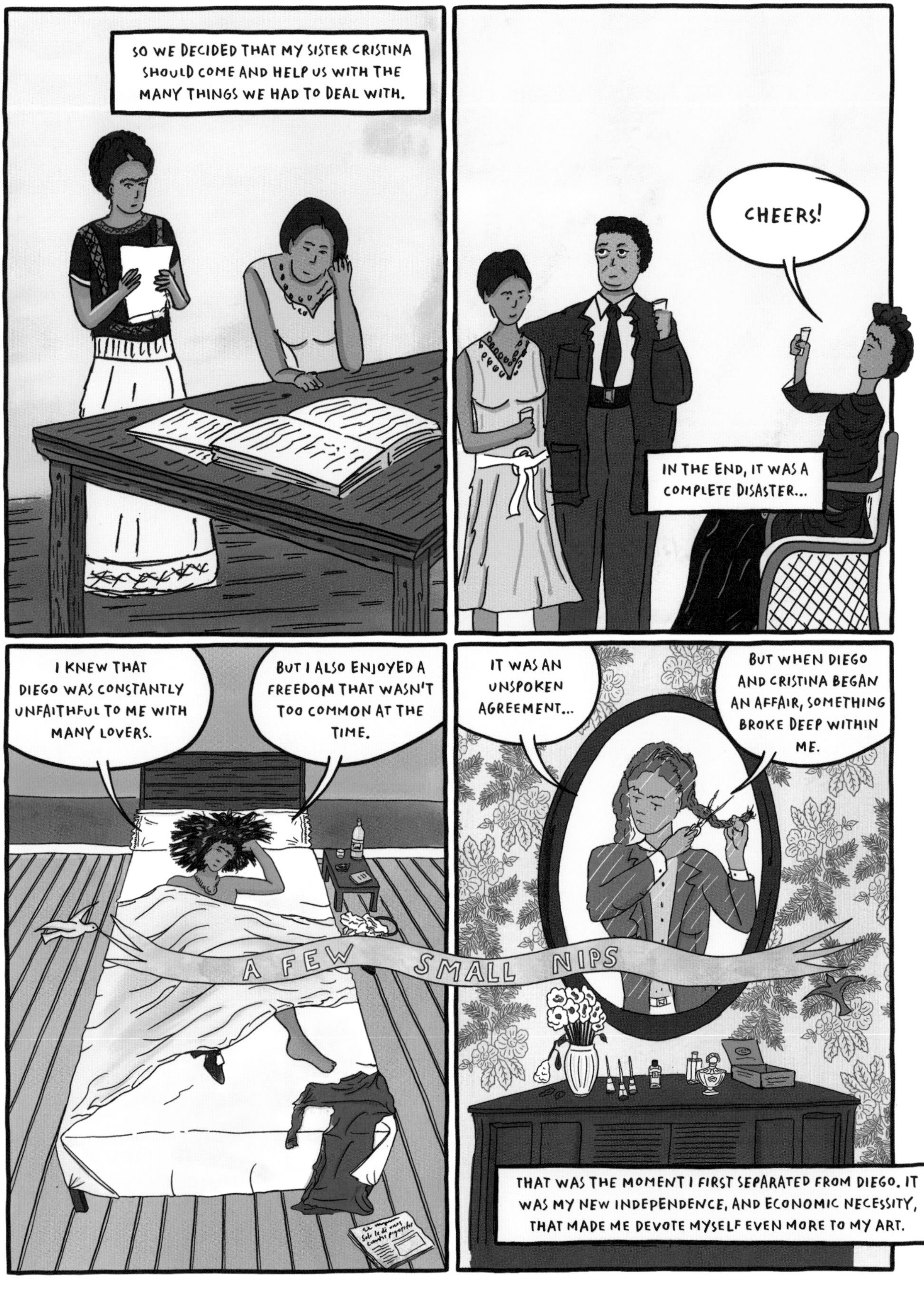
SO WE DECIDED THAT MY SISTER CRISTINA SHOULD COME AND HELP US WITH THE MANY THINGS WE HAD TO DEAL WITH.
CHEERS!
IN THE END, IT WAS A COMPLETE DISASTER...
I KNEW THAT DIEGO WAS CONSTANTLY UNFAITHFUL TO ME WITH MANY LOVERS.
BUT I ALSO ENJOYED A FREEDOM THAT WASN'T TOO COMMON AT THE TIME.
A FEW SMALL NIPS
IT WAS AN UNSPOKEN AGREEMENT...
BUT WHEN DIEGO AND CRISTINA BEGAN AN AFFAIR, SOMETHING BROKE DEEP WITHIN ME.
THAT WAS THE MOMENT I FIRST SEPARATED FROM DIEGO. IT WAS MY NEW INDEPENDENCE, AND ECONOMIC NECESSITY, THAT MADE ME DEVOTE MYSELF EVEN MORE TO MY ART.

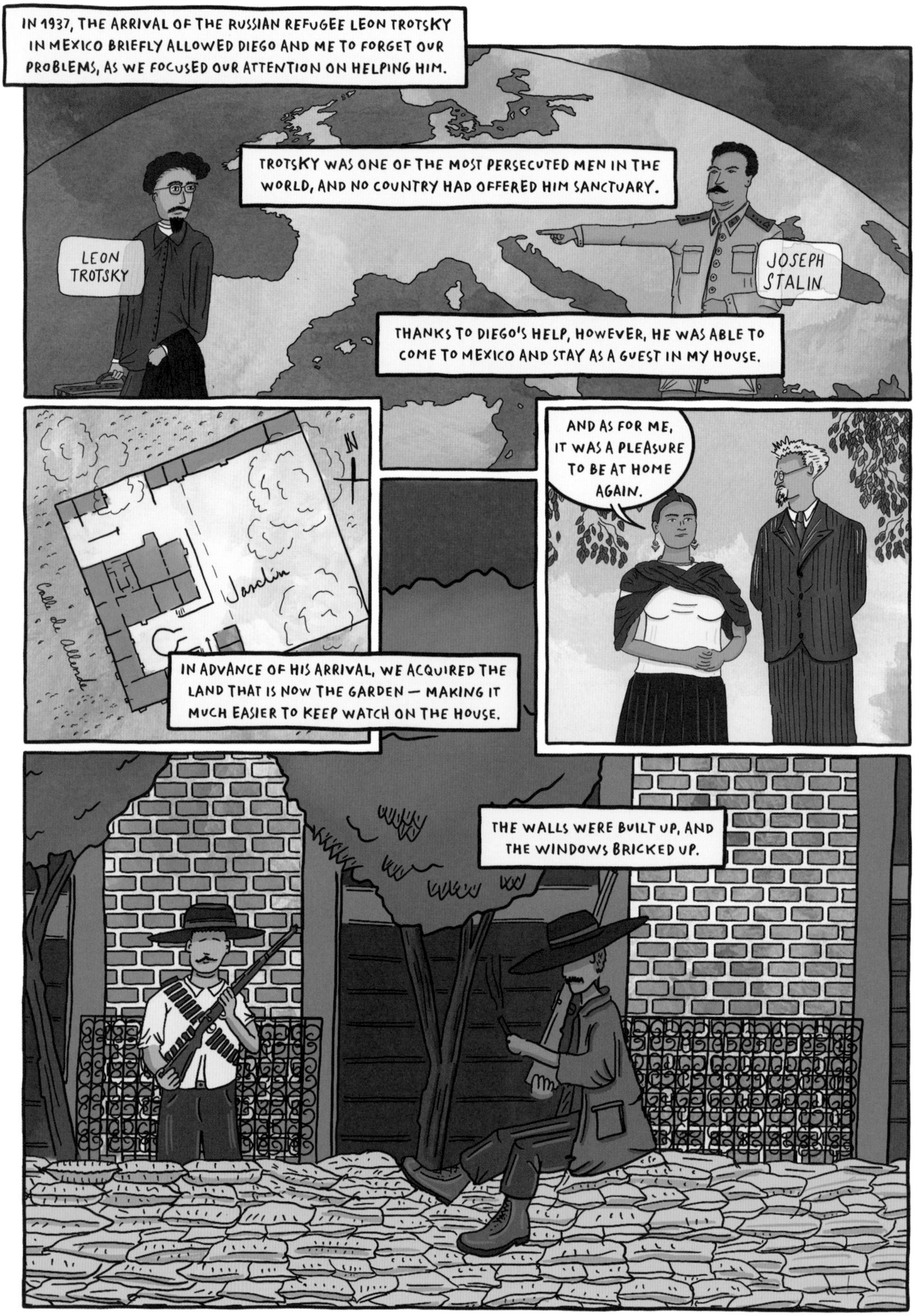

IN 1937, THE ARRIVAL OF THE RUSSIAN REFUGEE LEON TROTSKY IN MEXICO BRIEFLY ALLOWED DIEGO AND ME TO FORGET OUR PROBLEMS, AS WE FOCUSED OUR ATTENTION ON HELPING HIM.
TROTSKY WAS ONE OF THE MOST PERSECUTED MEN IN THE WORLD, AND NO COUNTRY HAD OFFERED HIM SANCTUARY.
LEON TROTSKY
JOSEPH STALIN
THANKS TO DIEGO'S HELP, HOWEVER, HE WAS ABLE TO COME TO MEXICO AND STAY AS A GUEST IN MY HOUSE.
N
Jardín
Calle de Allende
IN ADVANCE OF HIS ARRIVAL, WE ACQUIRED THE LAND THAT IS NOW THE GARDEN — MAKING IT MUCH EASIER TO KEEP WATCH ON THE HOUSE.
AND AS FOR ME, IT WAS A PLEASURE TO BE AT HOME AGAIN.
THE WALLS WERE BUILT UP, AND THE WINDOWS BRICKED UP.

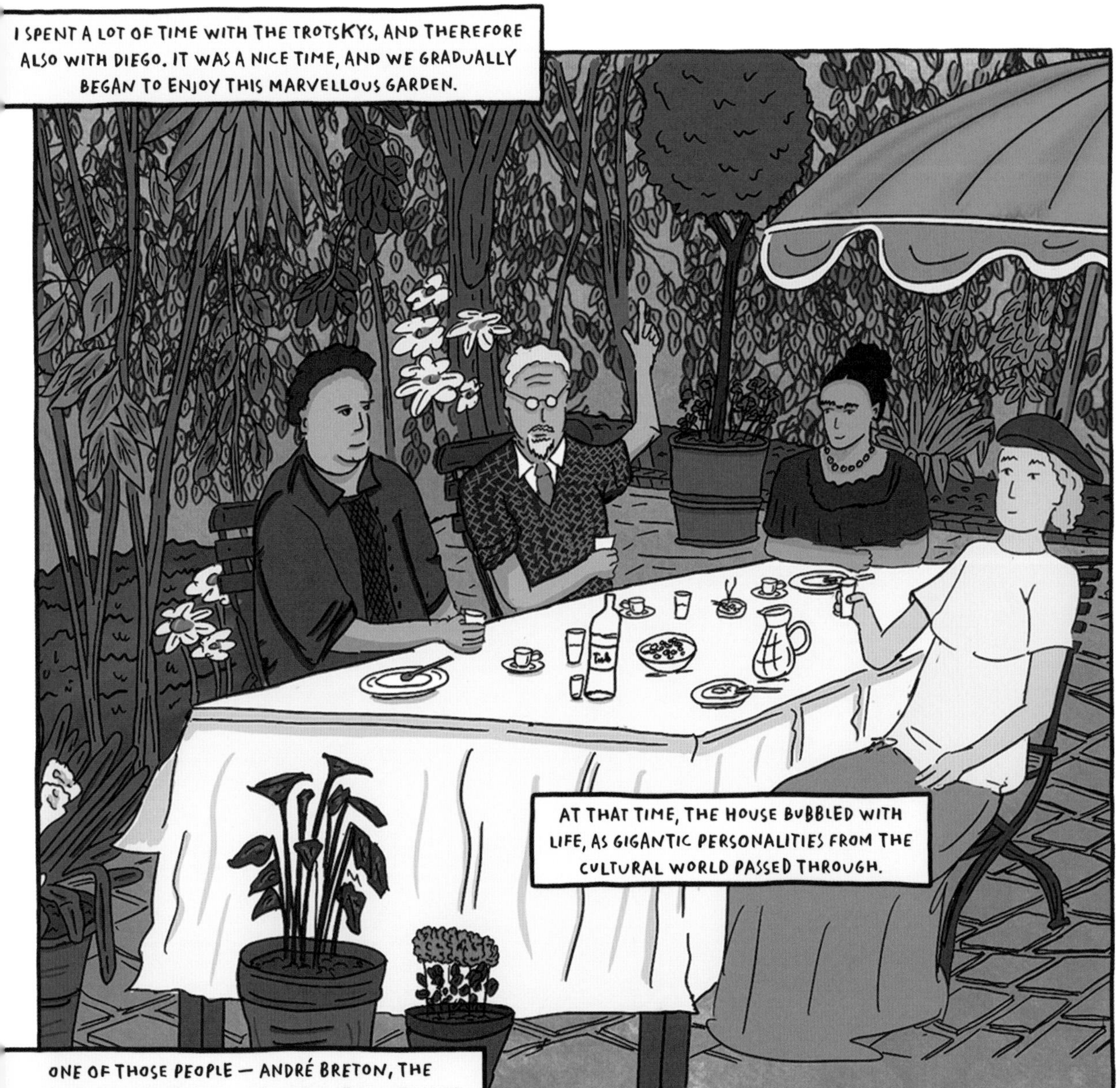
I SPENT A LOT OF TIME WITH THE TROTSKYS, AND THEREFORE ALSO WITH DIEGO. IT WAS A NICE TIME, AND WE GRADUALLY BEGAN TO ENJOY THIS MARVELLOUS GARDEN.
AT THAT TIME, THE HOUSE BUBBLED WITH LIFE, AS GIGANTIC PERSONALITIES FROM THE CULTURAL WORLD PASSED THROUGH.

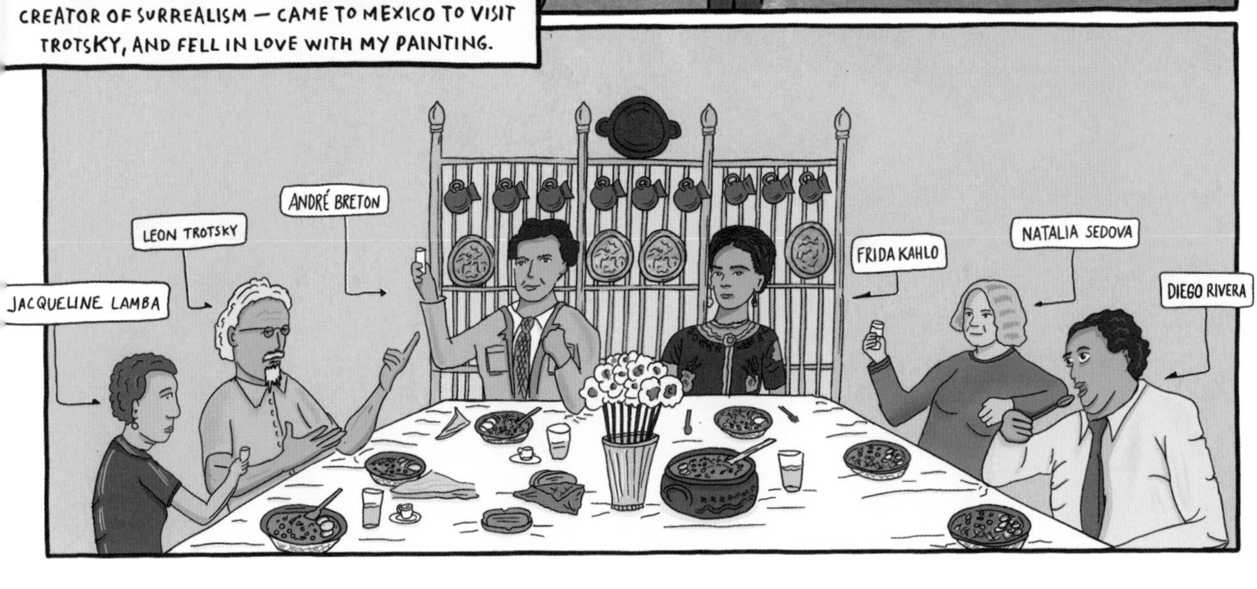
ONE OF THOSE PEOPLE — ANDRÉ BRETON, THE CREATOR OF SURREALISM — CAME TO MEXICO TO VISIT TROTSKY, AND FELL IN LOVE WITH MY PAINTING.
JACQUELINE LAMBA
LEON TROTSKY
ANDRÉ BRETON
FRIDA KAHLO
NATALIA SEDOVA
DIEGO RIVERA

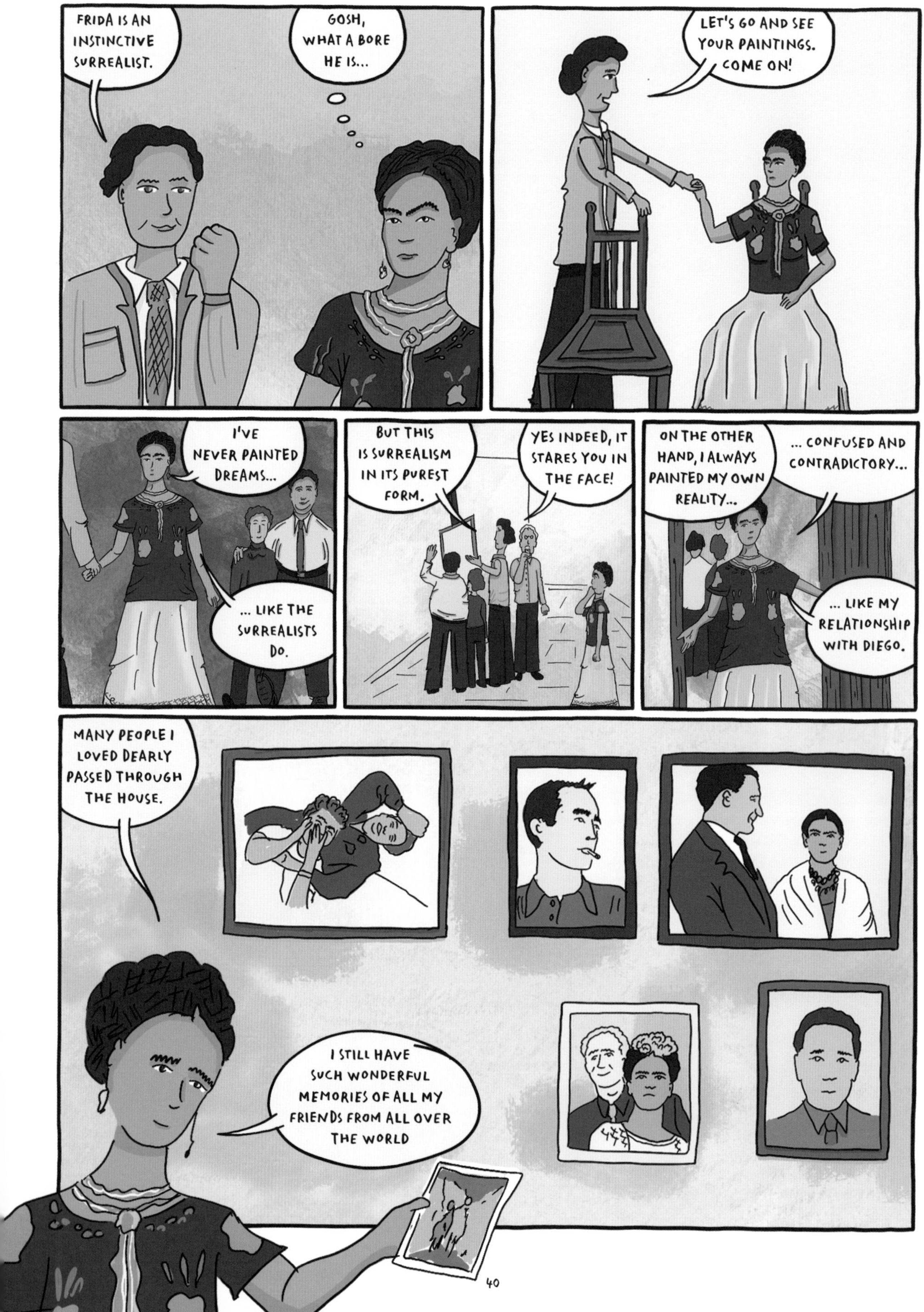
FRIDA IS AN INSTINCTIVE SURREALIST.
GOSH, WHAT A BORE HE IS...
LET'S GO AND SEE YOUR PAINTINGS. COME ON!
I'VE NEVER PAINTED DREAMS...
... LIKE THE SURREALISTS DO.
BUT THIS IS SURREALISM IN ITS PUREST FORM.
YES INDEED, IT STARES YOU IN THE FACE!
ON THE OTHER HAND, I ALWAYS PAINTED MY OWN REALITY...
... CONFUSED AND CONTRADICTORY...
... LIKE MY RELATIONSHIP WITH DIEGO.
MANY PEOPLE I LOVED DEARLY PASSED THROUGH THE HOUSE.
I STILL HAVE SUCH WONDERFUL MEMORIES OF ALL MY FRIENDS FROM ALL OVER THE WORLD

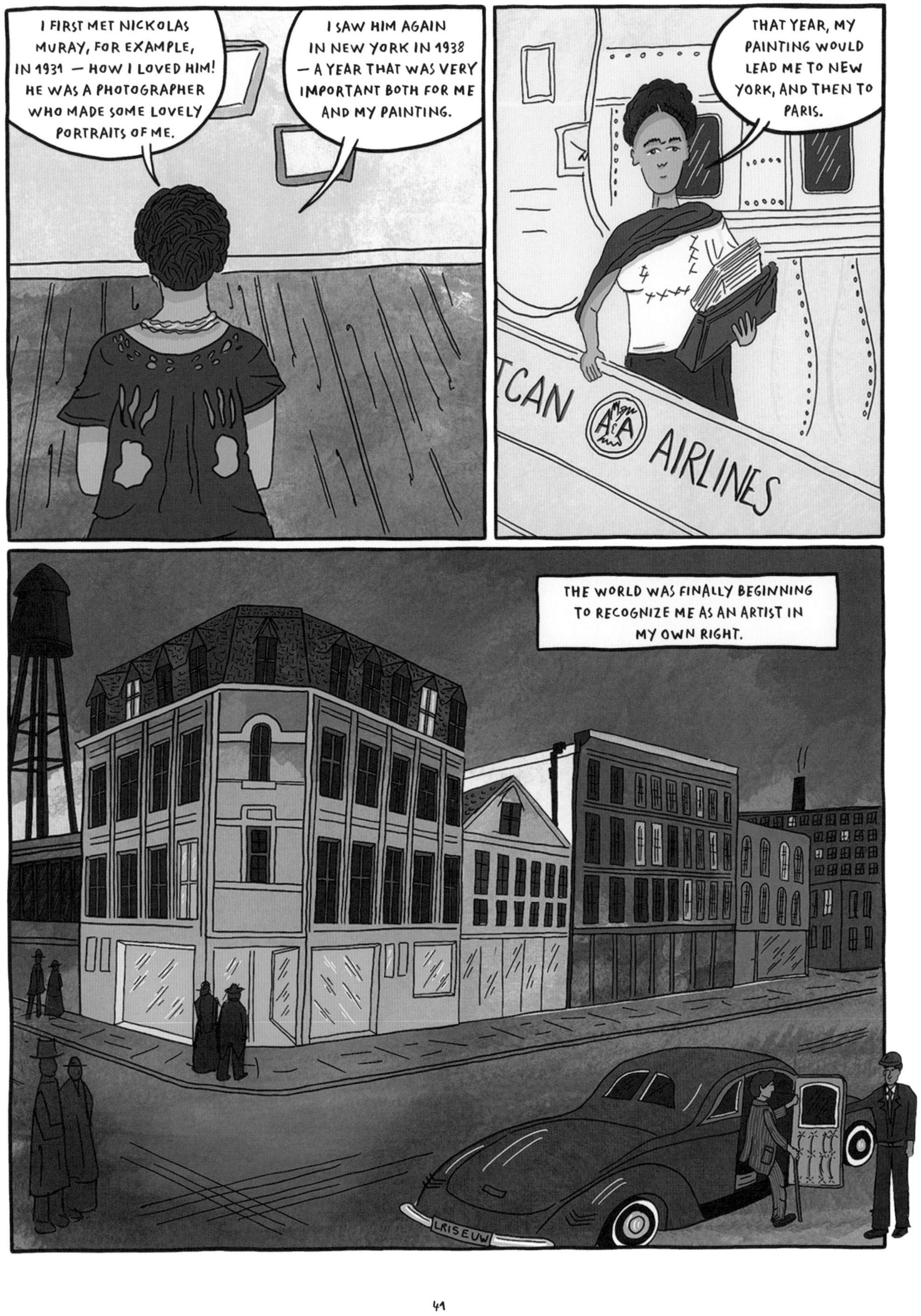
I FIRST MET NICKOLAS MURAY, FOR EXAMPLE, IN 1931 — HOW I LOVED HIM! HE WAS A PHOTOGRAPHER WHO MADE SOME LOVELY PORTRAITS OF ME.
I SAW HIM AGAIN IN NEW YORK IN 1938 — A YEAR THAT WAS VERY IMPORTANT BOTH FOR ME AND MY PAINTING.
THAT YEAR, MY PAINTING WOULD LEAD ME TO NEW YORK, AND THEN TO PARIS.
TCAN AIRLINES
THE WORLD WAS FINALLY BEGINNING TO RECOGNIZE ME AS AN ARTIST IN MY OWN RIGHT.
LRISEUW

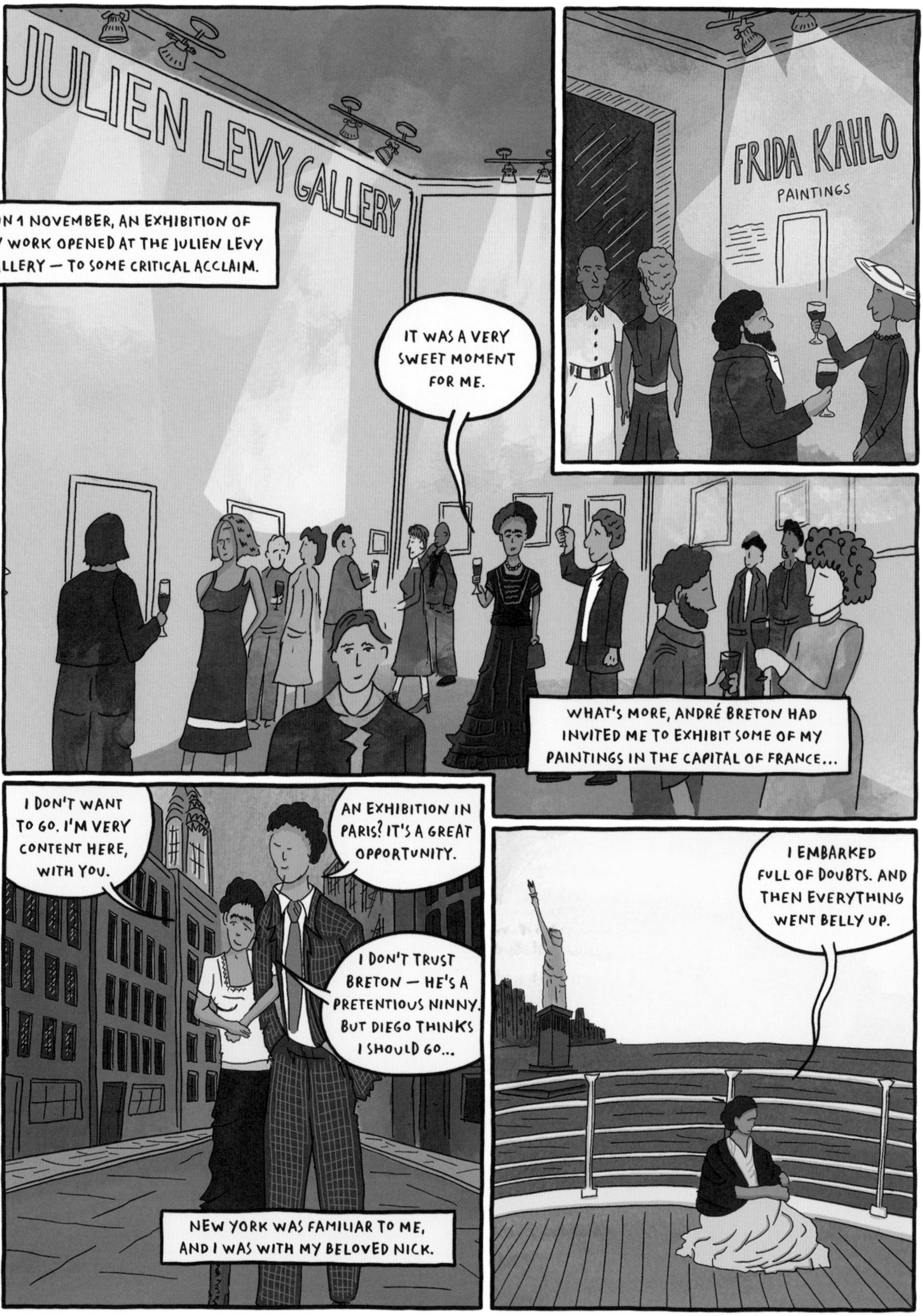
JULIEN LEVY GALLERY
ON 1 NOVEMBER, AN EXHIBITION OF MY WORK OPENED AT THE JULIEN LEVY GALLERY — TO SOME CRITICAL ACCLAIM.
IT WAS A VERY SWEET MOMENT FOR ME.
FRIDA KAHLO
PAINTINGS
WHAT'S MORE, ANDRÉ BRETON HAD INVITED ME TO EXHIBIT SOME OF MY PAINTINGS IN THE CAPITAL OF FRANCE...
AN EXHIBITION IN PARIS? IT'S A GREAT OPPORTUNITY.
I DON'T WANT TO GO. I'M VERY CONTENT HERE, WITH YOU.
I DON'T TRUST BRETON — HE'S A PRETENTIOUS NINNY. BUT DIEGO THINKS I SHOULD GO...
NEW YORK WAS FAMILIAR TO ME, AND I WAS WITH MY BELOVED NICK.
I EMBARKED FULL OF DOUBTS. AND THEN EVERYTHING WENT BELLY UP.

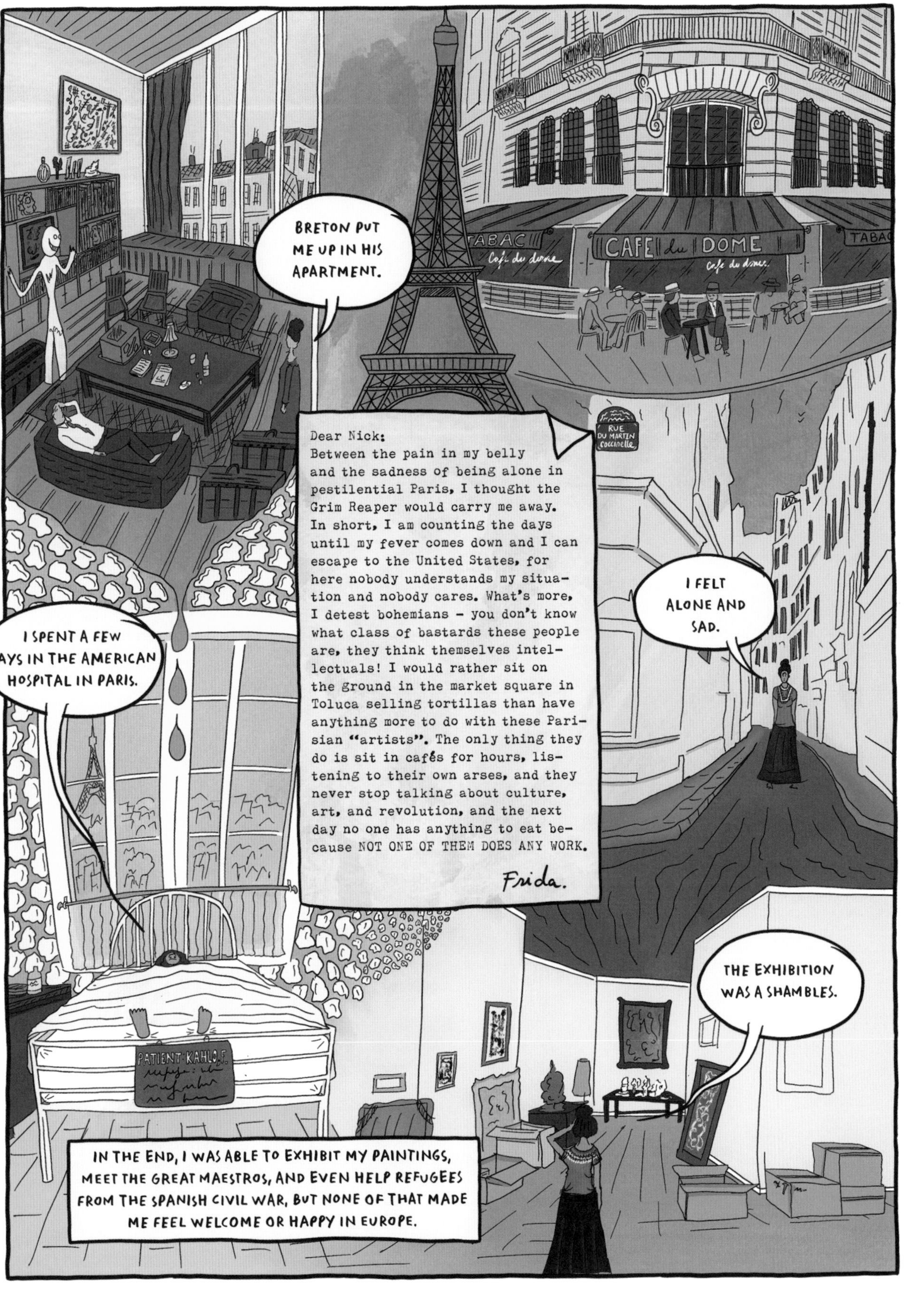
BRETON PUT ME UP IN HIS APARTMENT.
TABAC
Cafe du dome
CAFE du DOME
Cafe du dome
TABAC
RUE DU MARTIN coccinelle
Dear Nick:
Between the pain in my belly and the sadness of being alone in pestilential Paris, I thought the Grim Reaper would carry me away. In short, I am counting the days until my fever comes down and I can escape to the United States, for here nobody understands my situation and nobody cares. What's more, I detest bohemians - you don't know what class of bastards these people are, they think themselves intellectuals! I would rather sit on the ground in the market square in Toluca selling tortillas than have anything more to do with these Parisian "artists". The only thing they do is sit in cafés for hours, listening to their own arses, and they never stop talking about culture, art, and revolution, and the next day no one has anything to eat because NOT ONE OF THEM DOES ANY WORK.
Frida.
I SPENT A FEW DAYS IN THE AMERICAN HOSPITAL IN PARIS.
I FELT ALONE AND SAD.
PATIENT KAHLO, F.
THE EXHIBITION WAS A SHAMBLES.
IN THE END, I WAS ABLE TO EXHIBIT MY PAINTINGS, MEET THE GREAT MAESTROS, AND EVEN HELP REFUGEES FROM THE SPANISH CIVIL WAR, BUT NONE OF THAT MADE ME FEEL WELCOME OR HAPPY IN EUROPE.

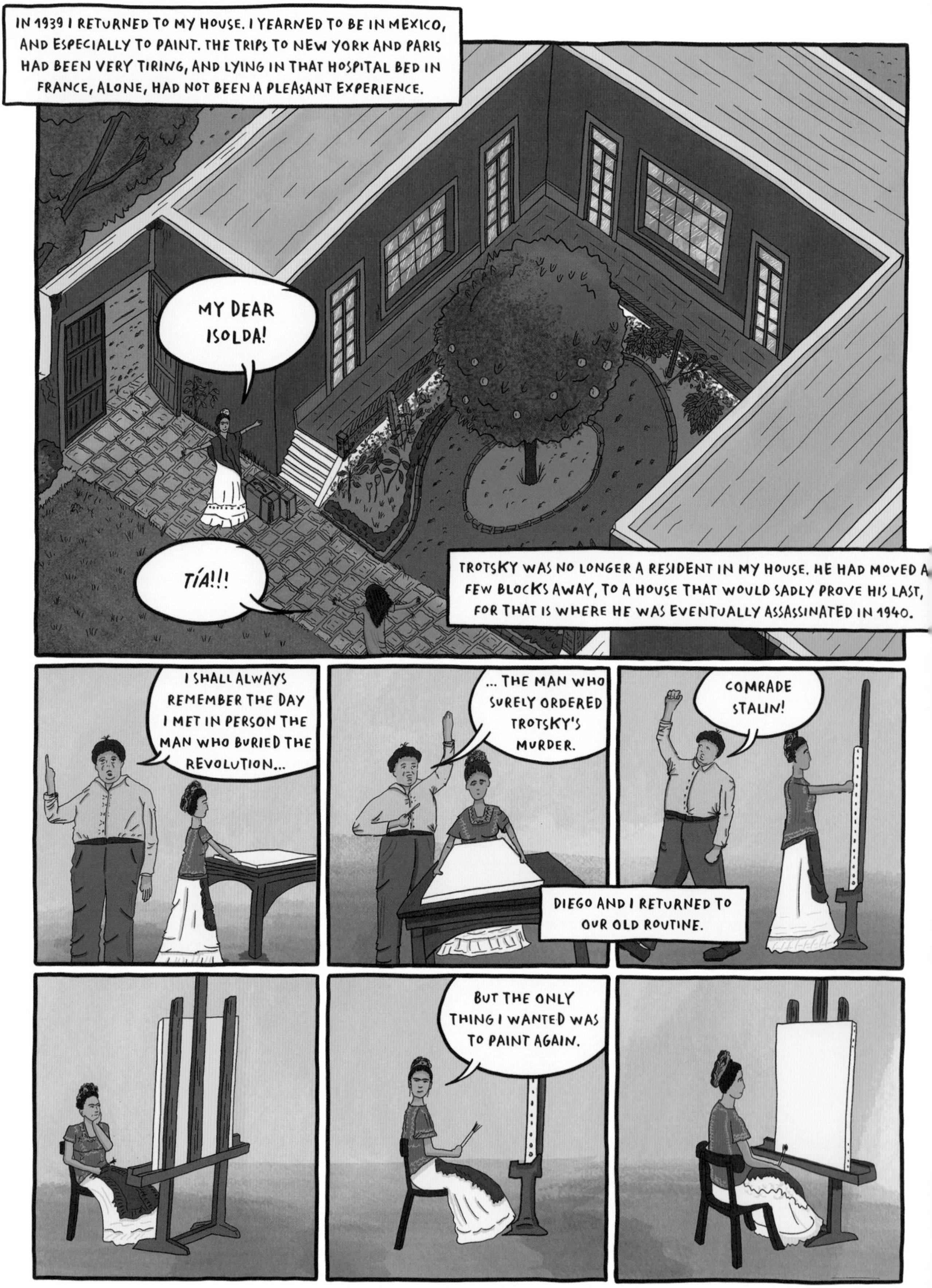
IN 1939 I RETURNED TO MY HOUSE. I YEARNED TO BE IN MEXICO, AND ESPECIALLY TO PAINT. THE TRIPS TO NEW YORK AND PARIS HAD BEEN VERY TIRING, AND LYING IN THAT HOSPITAL BED IN FRANCE, ALONE, HAD NOT BEEN A PLEASANT EXPERIENCE.
MY DEAR ISOLDA!
TÍA!!!
TROTSKY WAS NO LONGER A RESIDENT IN MY HOUSE. HE HAD MOVED A FEW BLOCKS AWAY, TO A HOUSE THAT WOULD SADLY PROVE HIS LAST, FOR THAT IS WHERE HE WAS EVENTUALLY ASSASSINATED IN 1940.
I SHALL ALWAYS REMEMBER THE DAY I MET IN PERSON THE MAN WHO BURIED THE REVOLUTION...
... THE MAN WHO SURELY ORDERED TROTSKY'S MURDER.
COMRADE STALIN!
DIEGO AND I RETURNED TO OUR OLD ROUTINE.
BUT THE ONLY THING I WANTED WAS TO PAINT AGAIN.

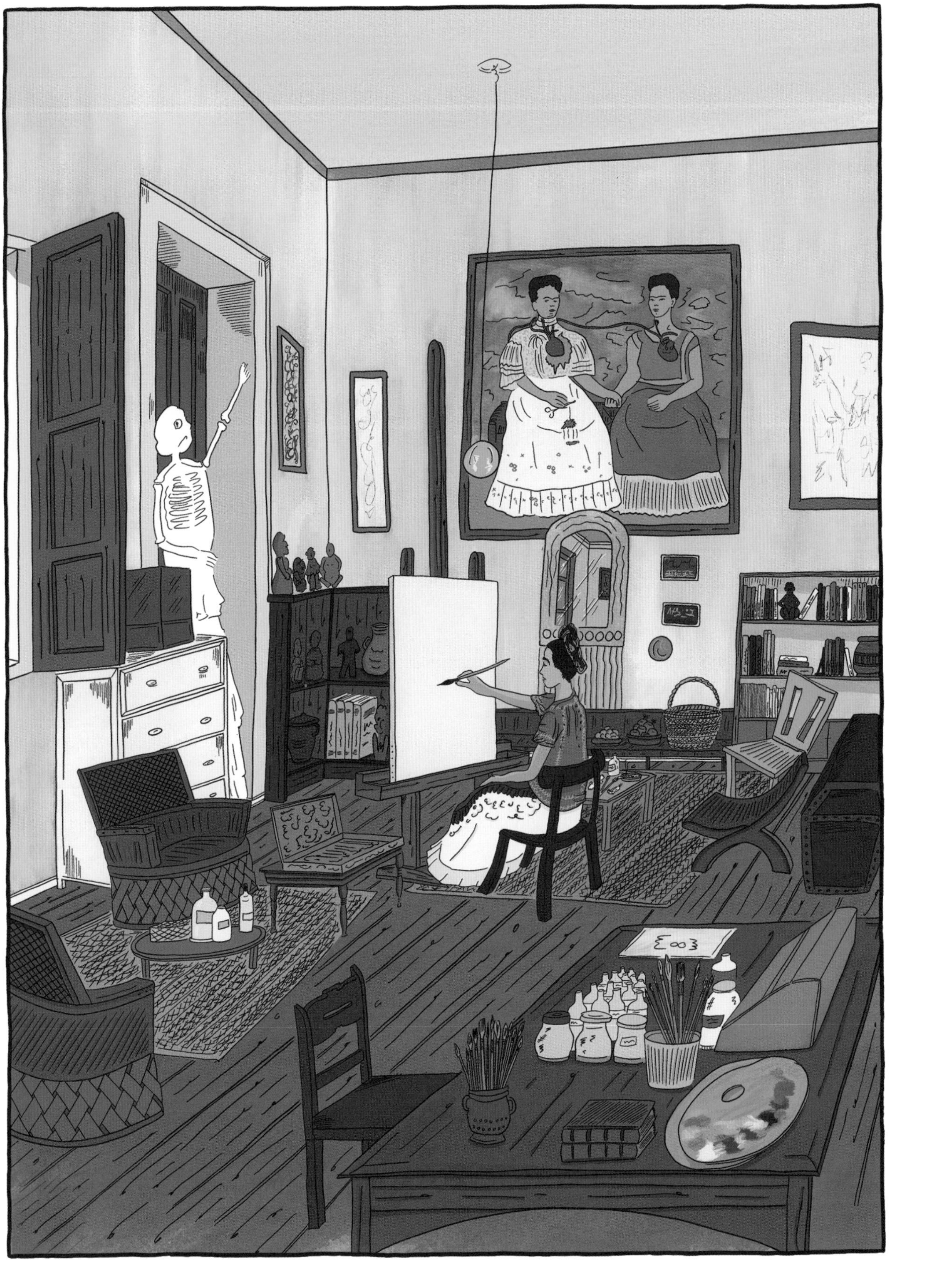

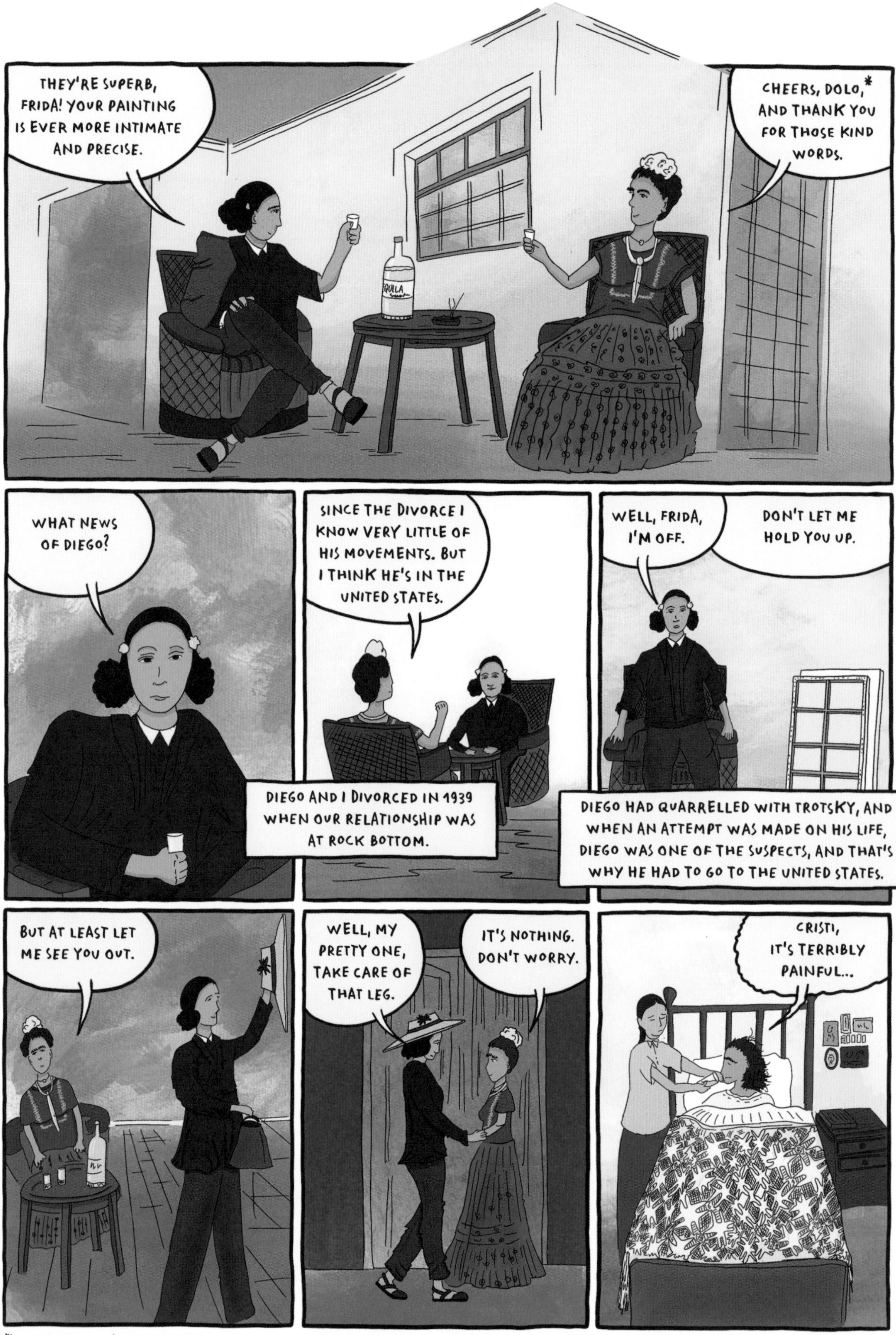
THEY'RE SUPERB, FRIDA! YOUR PAINTING IS EVER MORE INTIMATE AND PRECISE.
CHEERS, DOLO,* AND THANK YOU FOR THOSE KIND WORDS.
WHAT NEWS OF DIEGO?
SINCE THE DIVORCE I KNOW VERY LITTLE OF HIS MOVEMENTS. BUT I THINK HE'S IN THE UNITED STATES.
DIEGO AND I DIVORCED IN 1939 WHEN OUR RELATIONSHIP WAS AT ROCK BOTTOM.
WELL, FRIDA, I'M OFF.
DON'T LET ME HOLD YOU UP.
DIEGO HAD QUARRELLED WITH TROTSKY, AND WHEN AN ATTEMPT WAS MADE ON HIS LIFE, DIEGO WAS ONE OF THE SUSPECTS, AND THAT'S WHY HE HAD TO GO TO THE UNITED STATES.
BUT AT LEAST LET ME SEE YOU OUT.
WELL, MY PRETTY ONE, TAKE CARE OF THAT LEG.
IT'S NOTHING. DON'T WORRY.
CRISTI, IT'S TERRIBLY PAINFUL...

* DOLORES DEL RÍO (FILM STAR).

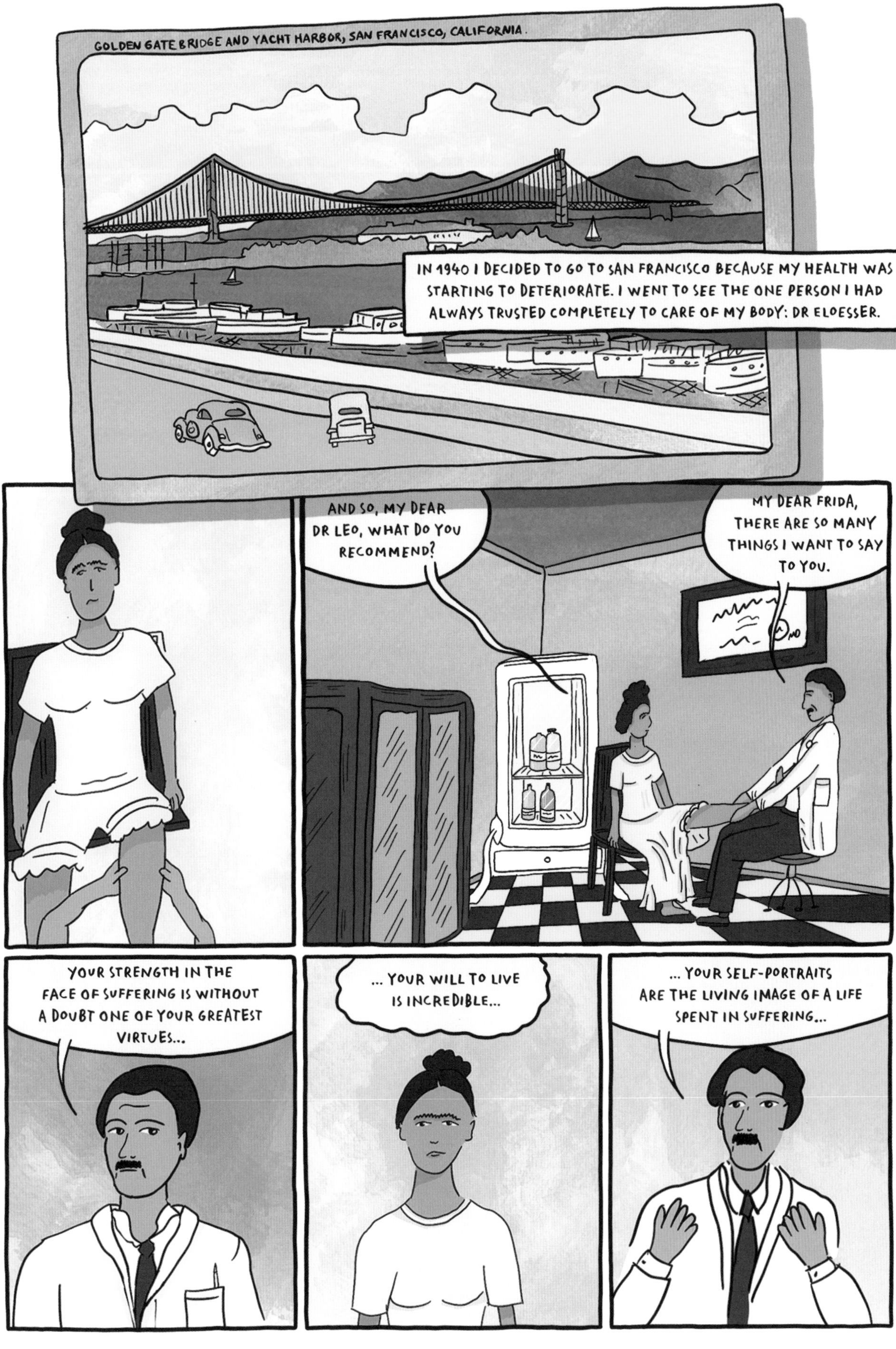
GOLDEN GATE BRIDGE AND YACHT HARBOR, SAN FRANCISCO, CALIFORNIA.
IN 1940 I DECIDED TO GO TO SAN FRANCISCO BECAUSE MY HEALTH WAS STARTING TO DETERIORATE. I WENT TO SEE THE ONE PERSON I HAD ALWAYS TRUSTED COMPLETELY TO CARE OF MY BODY: DR ELOESSER.
AND SO, MY DEAR DR LEO, WHAT DO YOU RECOMMEND?
MY DEAR FRIDA, THERE ARE SO MANY THINGS I WANT TO SAY TO YOU.
YOUR STRENGTH IN THE FACE OF SUFFERING IS WITHOUT A DOUBT ONE OF YOUR GREATEST VIRTUES...
... YOUR WILL TO LIVE IS INCREDIBLE...
... YOUR SELF-PORTRAITS ARE THE LIVING IMAGE OF A LIFE SPENT IN SUFFERING...

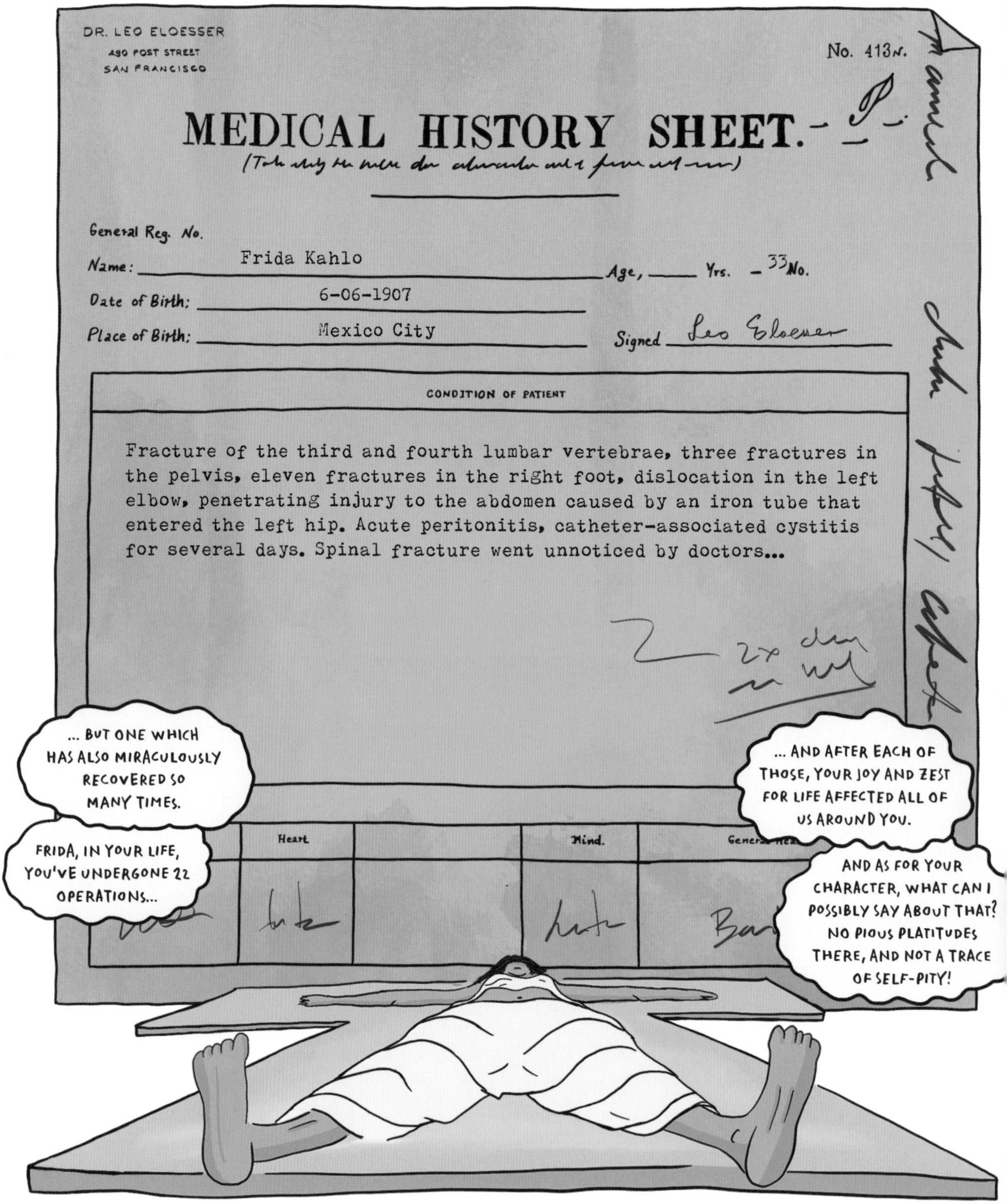


*To feel in my own pain the pain of those who suffer, and to find encouragement in the necessity of living in order to fight for them.*

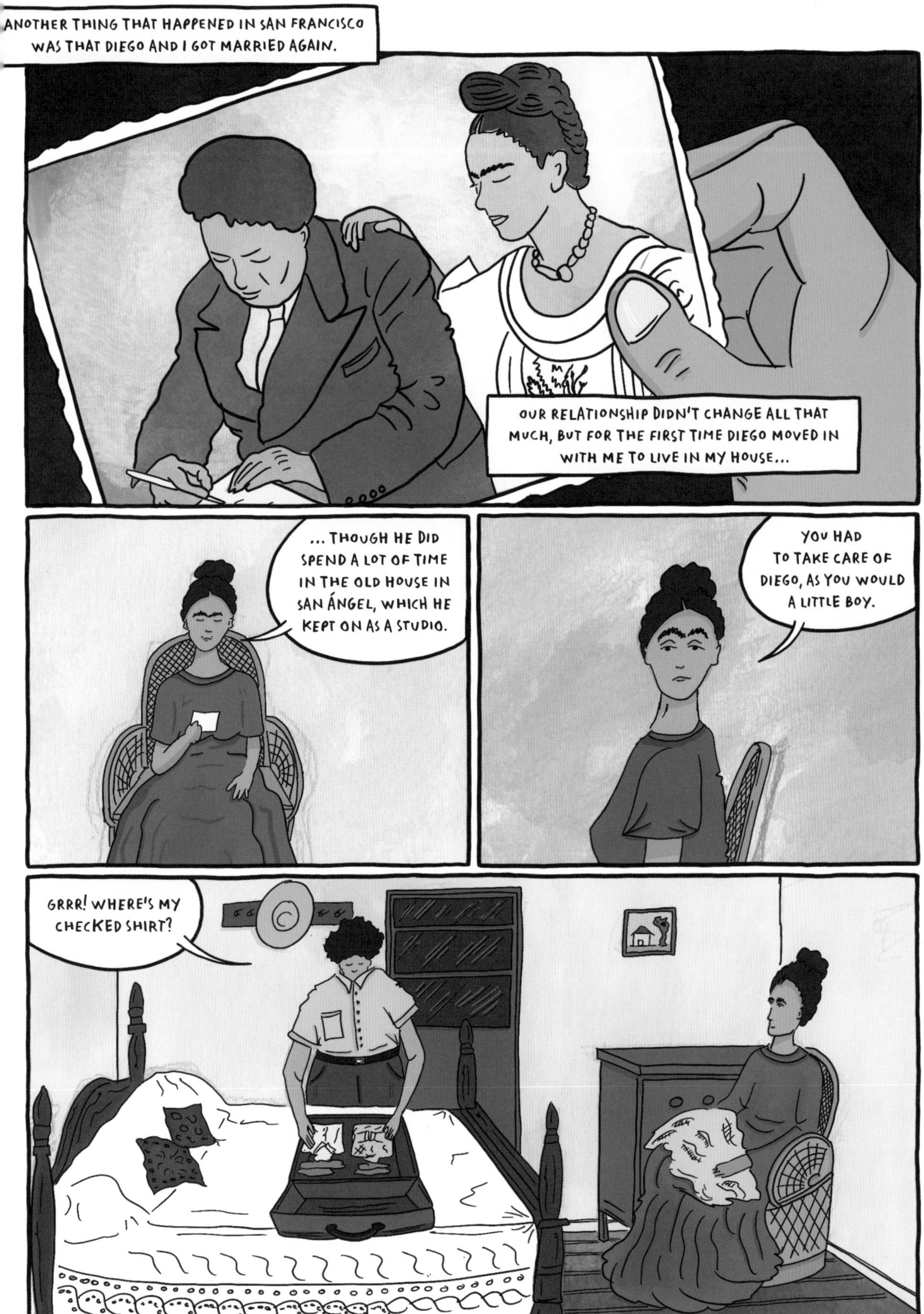
ANOTHER THING THAT HAPPENED IN SAN FRANCISCO WAS THAT DIEGO AND I GOT MARRIED AGAIN.
OUR RELATIONSHIP DIDN'T CHANGE ALL THAT MUCH, BUT FOR THE FIRST TIME DIEGO MOVED IN WITH ME TO LIVE IN MY HOUSE...
... THOUGH HE DID SPEND A LOT OF TIME IN THE OLD HOUSE IN SAN ÁNGEL, WHICH HE KEPT ON AS A STUDIO.
YOU HAD TO TAKE CARE OF DIEGO, AS YOU WOULD A LITTLE BOY.
GRRR! WHERE'S MY CHECKED SHIRT?

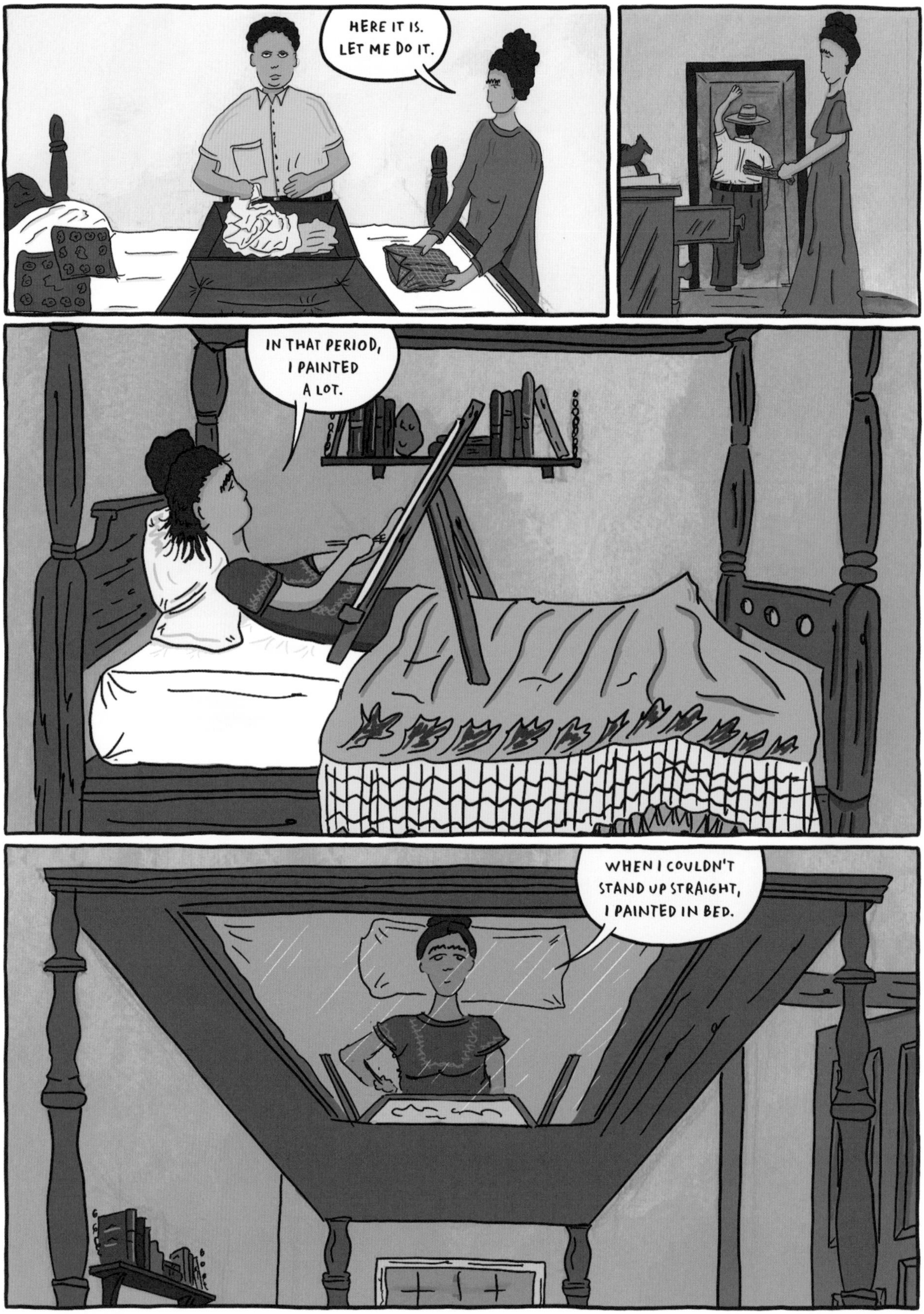
HERE IT IS. LET ME DO IT.
IN THAT PERIOD, I PAINTED A LOT.
WHEN I COULDN'T STAND UP STRAIGHT, I PAINTED IN BED.

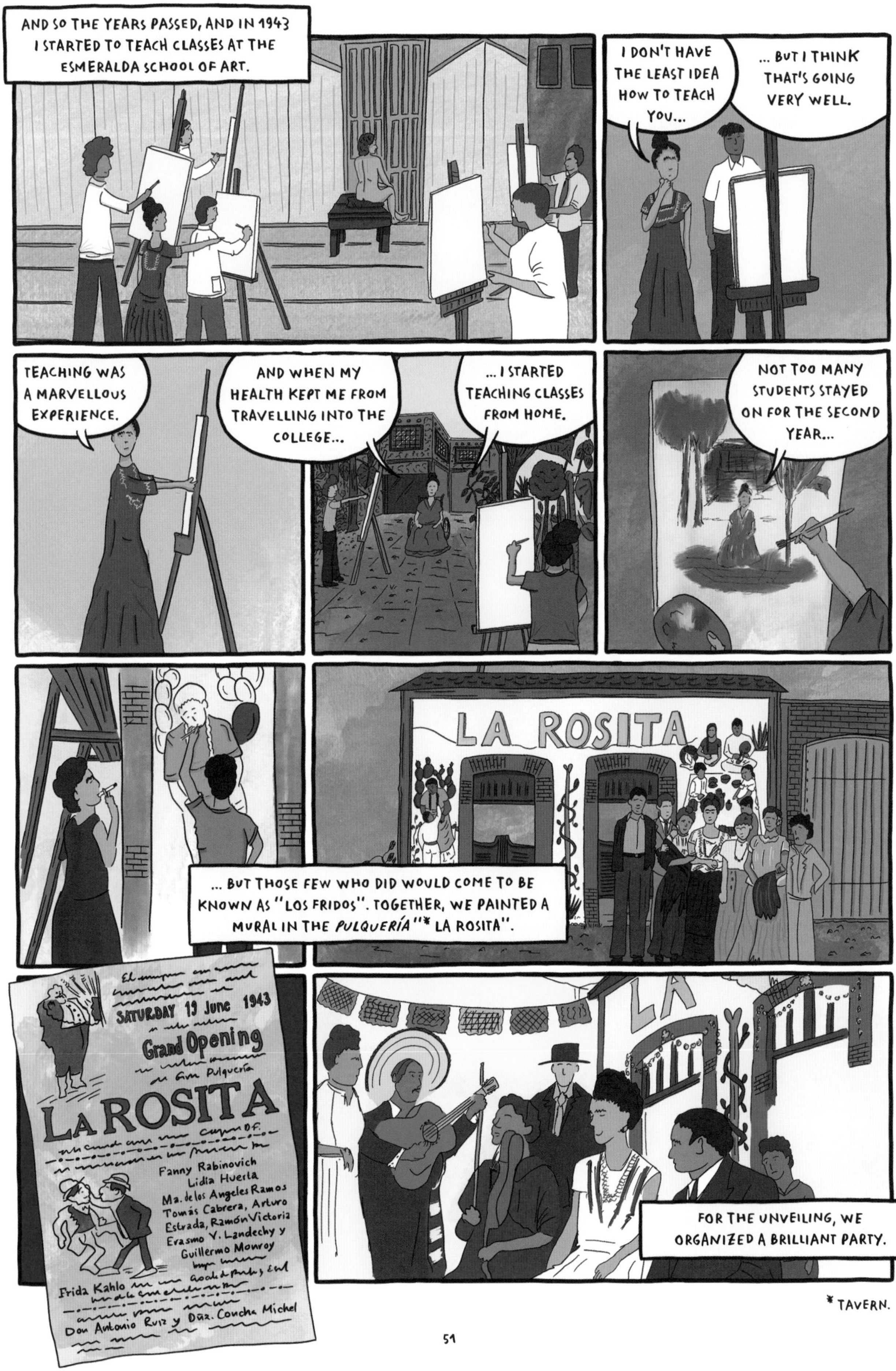
AND SO THE YEARS PASSED, AND IN 1943 I STARTED TO TEACH CLASSES AT THE ESMERALDA SCHOOL OF ART.
I DON'T HAVE THE LEAST IDEA HOW TO TEACH YOU...
... BUT I THINK THAT'S GOING VERY WELL.
TEACHING WAS A MARVELLOUS EXPERIENCE.
AND WHEN MY HEALTH KEPT ME FROM TRAVELLING INTO THE COLLEGE...
... I STARTED TEACHING CLASSES FROM HOME.
NOT TOO MANY STUDENTS STAYED ON FOR THE SECOND YEAR...
LA ROSITA
... BUT THOSE FEW WHO DID WOULD COME TO BE KNOWN AS "LOS FRIDOS". TOGETHER, WE PAINTED A MURAL IN THE *PULQUERÍA*"* LA ROSITA".
SATURDAY 19 June 1943
Grand Opening
Pulquería
LA ROSITA
D.F.
Fanny Rabinovich
Lidia Huerta
Ma. de los Angeles Ramos
Tomás Cabrera, Arturo
Estrada, Ramón Victoria
Erasmo V. Landechy y
Guillermo Monroy
Frida Kahlo
Don Antonio Ruiz y Díaz. Concha Michel
LA
FOR THE UNVEILING, WE ORGANIZED A BRILLIANT PARTY.

* TAVERN.

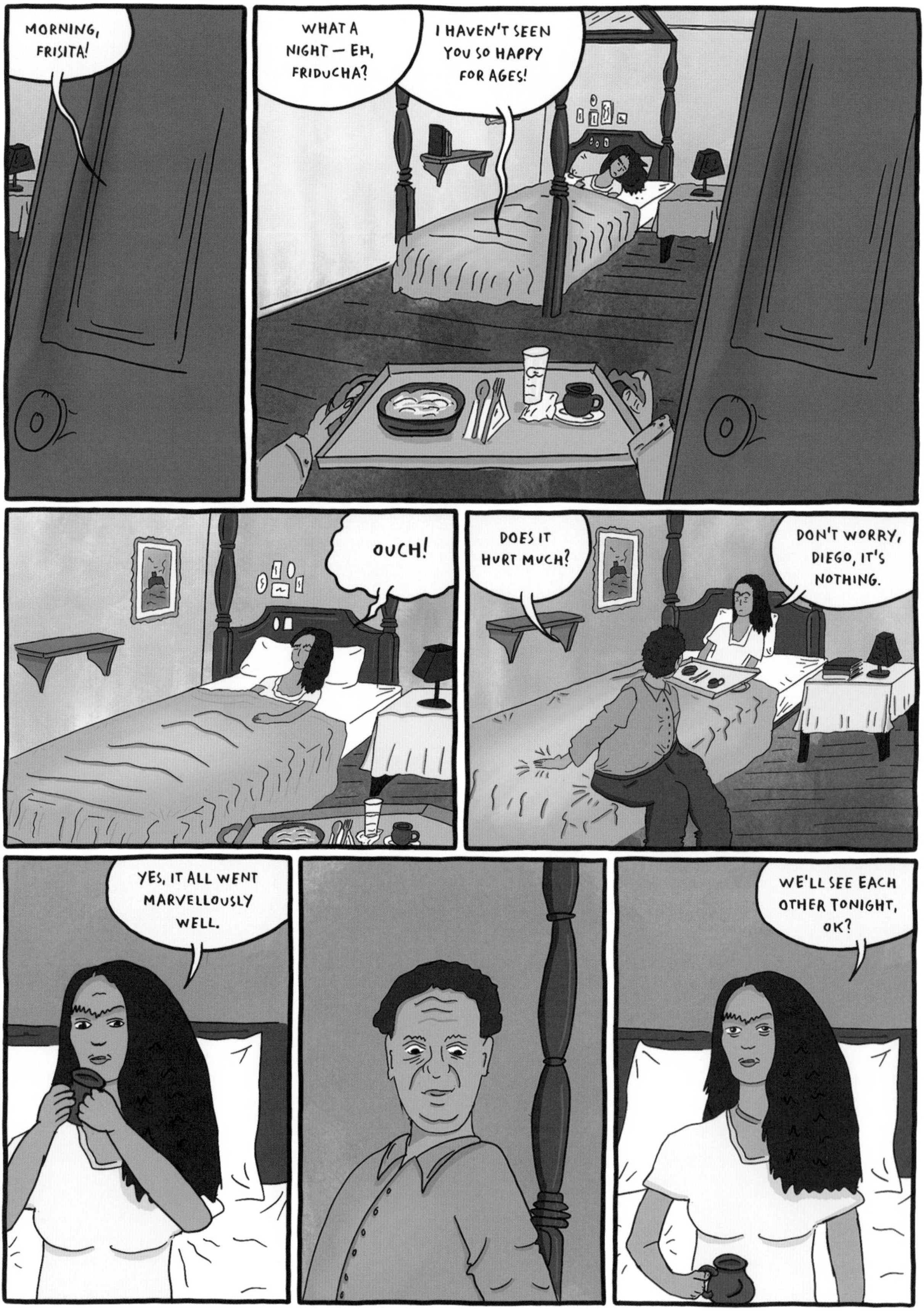
MORNING, FRISITA!
WHAT A NIGHT — EH, FRIDUCHA?
I HAVEN'T SEEN YOU SO HAPPY FOR AGES!
OUCH!
DOES IT HURT MUCH?
DON'T WORRY, DIEGO, IT'S NOTHING.
YES, IT ALL WENT MARVELLOUSLY WELL.
WE'LL SEE EACH OTHER TONIGHT, OK?

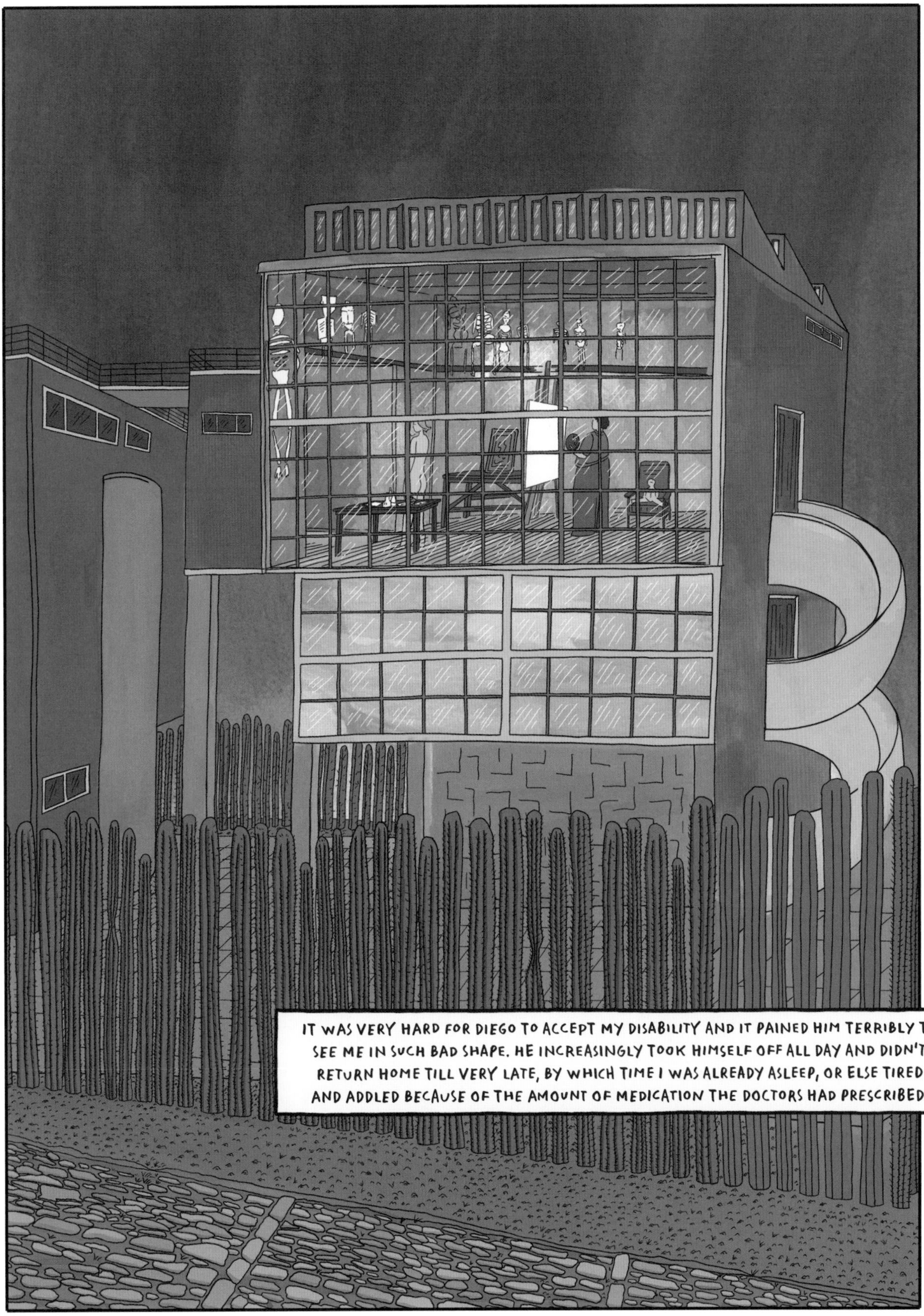
IT WAS VERY HARD FOR DIEGO TO ACCEPT MY DISABILITY AND IT PAINED HIM TERRIBLY TO SEE ME IN SUCH BAD SHAPE. HE INCREASINGLY TOOK HIMSELF OFF ALL DAY AND DIDN'T RETURN HOME TILL VERY LATE, BY WHICH TIME I WAS ALREADY ASLEEP, OR ELSE TIRED AND ADDLED BECAUSE OF THE AMOUNT OF MEDICATION THE DOCTORS HAD PRESCRIBED.

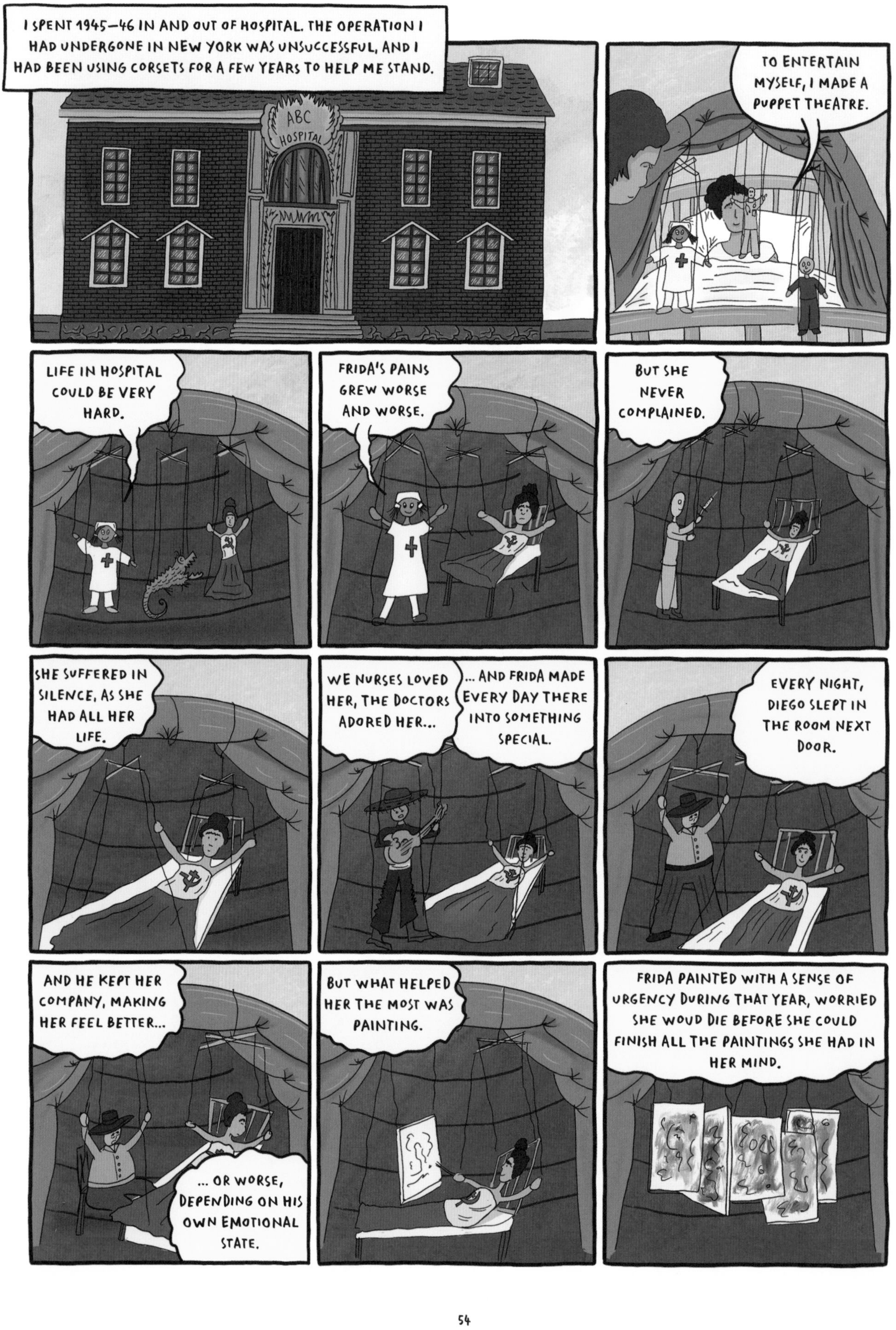
I SPENT 1945–46 IN AND OUT OF HOSPITAL. THE OPERATION I HAD UNDERGONE IN NEW YORK WAS UNSUCCESSFUL, AND I HAD BEEN USING CORSETS FOR A FEW YEARS TO HELP ME STAND.
ABC HOSPITAL
TO ENTERTAIN MYSELF, I MADE A PUPPET THEATRE.
LIFE IN HOSPITAL COULD BE VERY HARD.
FRIDA'S PAINS GREW WORSE AND WORSE.
BUT SHE NEVER COMPLAINED.
SHE SUFFERED IN SILENCE, AS SHE HAD ALL HER LIFE.
WE NURSES LOVED HER, THE DOCTORS ADORED HER...
... AND FRIDA MADE EVERY DAY THERE INTO SOMETHING SPECIAL.
EVERY NIGHT, DIEGO SLEPT IN THE ROOM NEXT DOOR.
AND HE KEPT HER COMPANY, MAKING HER FEEL BETTER...
... OR WORSE, DEPENDING ON HIS OWN EMOTIONAL STATE.
BUT WHAT HELPED HER THE MOST WAS PAINTING.
FRIDA PAINTED WITH A SENSE OF URGENCY DURING THAT YEAR, WORRIED SHE WOUD DIE BEFORE SHE COULD FINISH ALL THE PAINTINGS SHE HAD IN HER MIND.

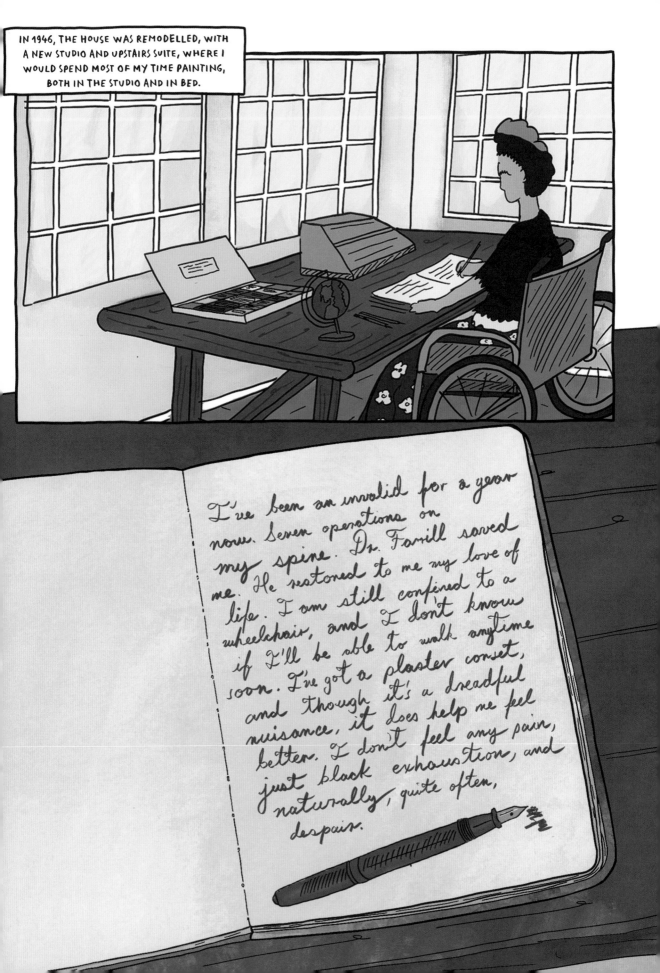

IN 1946, THE HOUSE WAS REMODELLED, WITH A NEW STUDIO AND UPSTAIRS SUITE, WHERE I WOULD SPEND MOST OF MY TIME PAINTING, BOTH IN THE STUDIO AND IN BED.

I've been an invalid for a year now. Seven operations on my spine. Dr. Farill saved me. He restored to me my love of life. I am still confined to a wheelchair, and I don't know if I'll be able to walk anytime soon. I've got a plaster corset, and though it's a dreadful nuisance, it does help me feel better. I don't feel any pain, just black exhaustion, and naturally, quite often, despair.

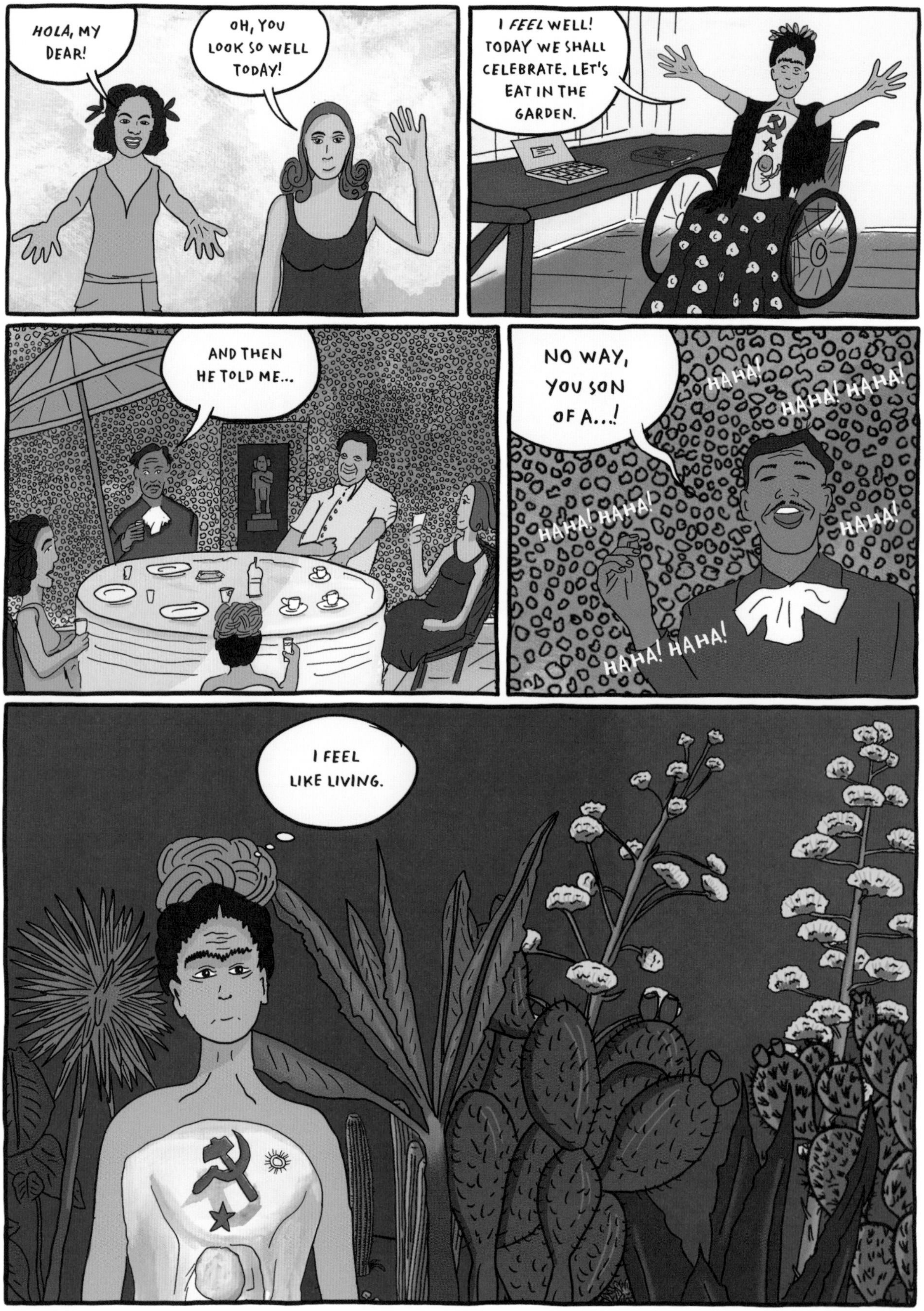
HOLA, MY DEAR!
OH, YOU LOOK SO WELL TODAY!
I FEEL WELL! TODAY WE SHALL CELEBRATE. LET'S EAT IN THE GARDEN.
AND THEN HE TOLD ME...
NO WAY, YOU SON OF A...!
HAHA! HAHA! HAHA! HAHA! HAHA! HAHA! HAHA! HAHA! HAHA!
I FEEL LIKE LIVING.

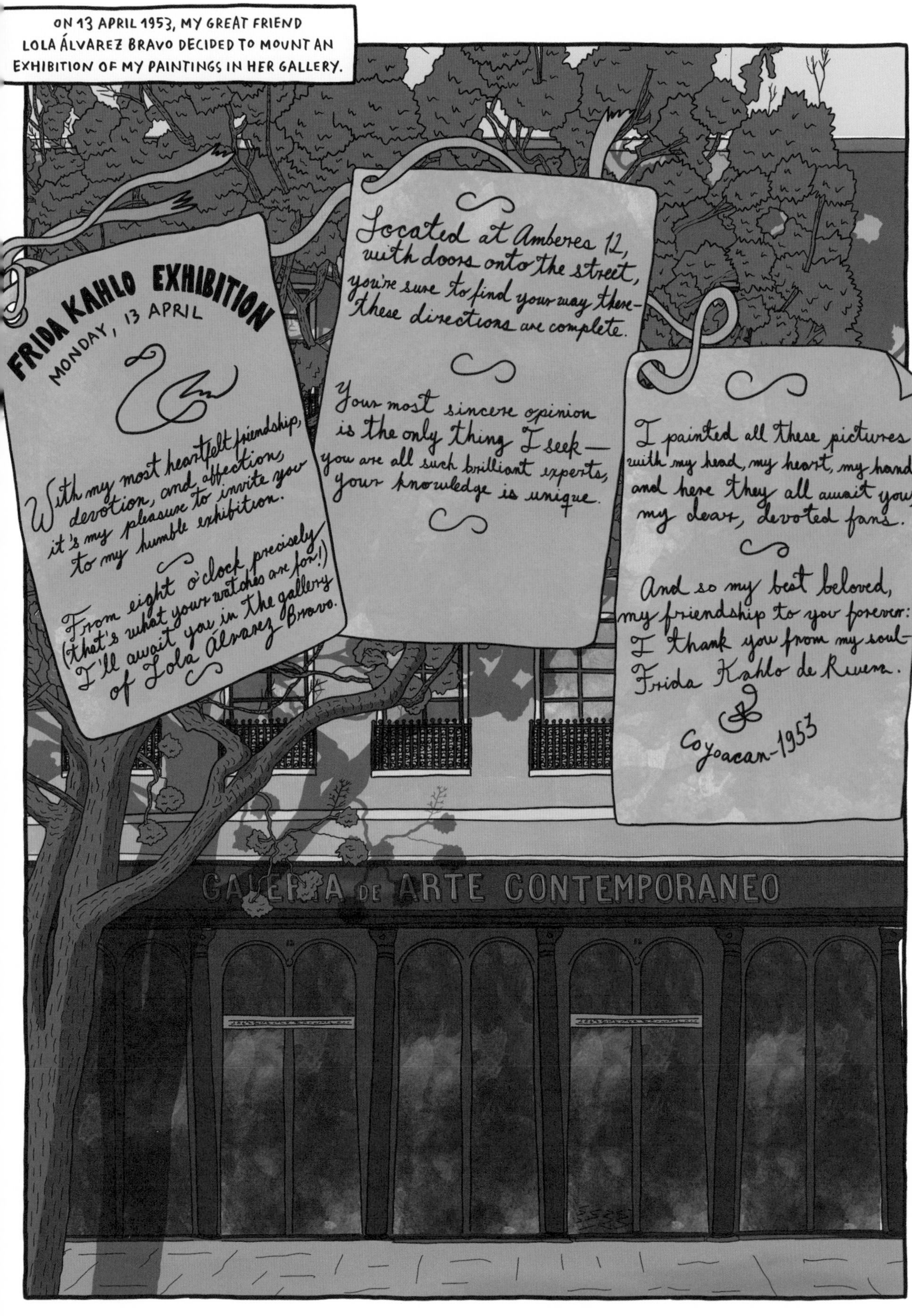
ON 13 APRIL 1953, MY GREAT FRIEND LOLA ÁLVAREZ BRAVO DECIDED TO MOUNT AN EXHIBITION OF MY PAINTINGS IN HER GALLERY.
FRIDA KAHLO EXHIBITION
MONDAY, 13 APRIL
With my most heartfelt friendship, devotion, and affection, it's my pleasure to invite you to my humble exhibition.
From eight o'clock precisely (that's what your watches are for!) I'll await you in the gallery of Lola Álvarez Bravo.
Located at Amberes 12, with doors onto the street, you're sure to find your way there - these directions are complete.
Your most sincere opinion is the only thing I seek— you are all such brilliant experts, your knowledge is unique.
I painted all these pictures with my head, my heart, my hands, and here they all await you, my dear, devoted fans.
And so my best beloved, my friendship to you forever: I thank you from my soul - Frida Kahlo de Rivera.
Coyoacan-1953
GALERIA DE ARTE CONTEMPORANEO

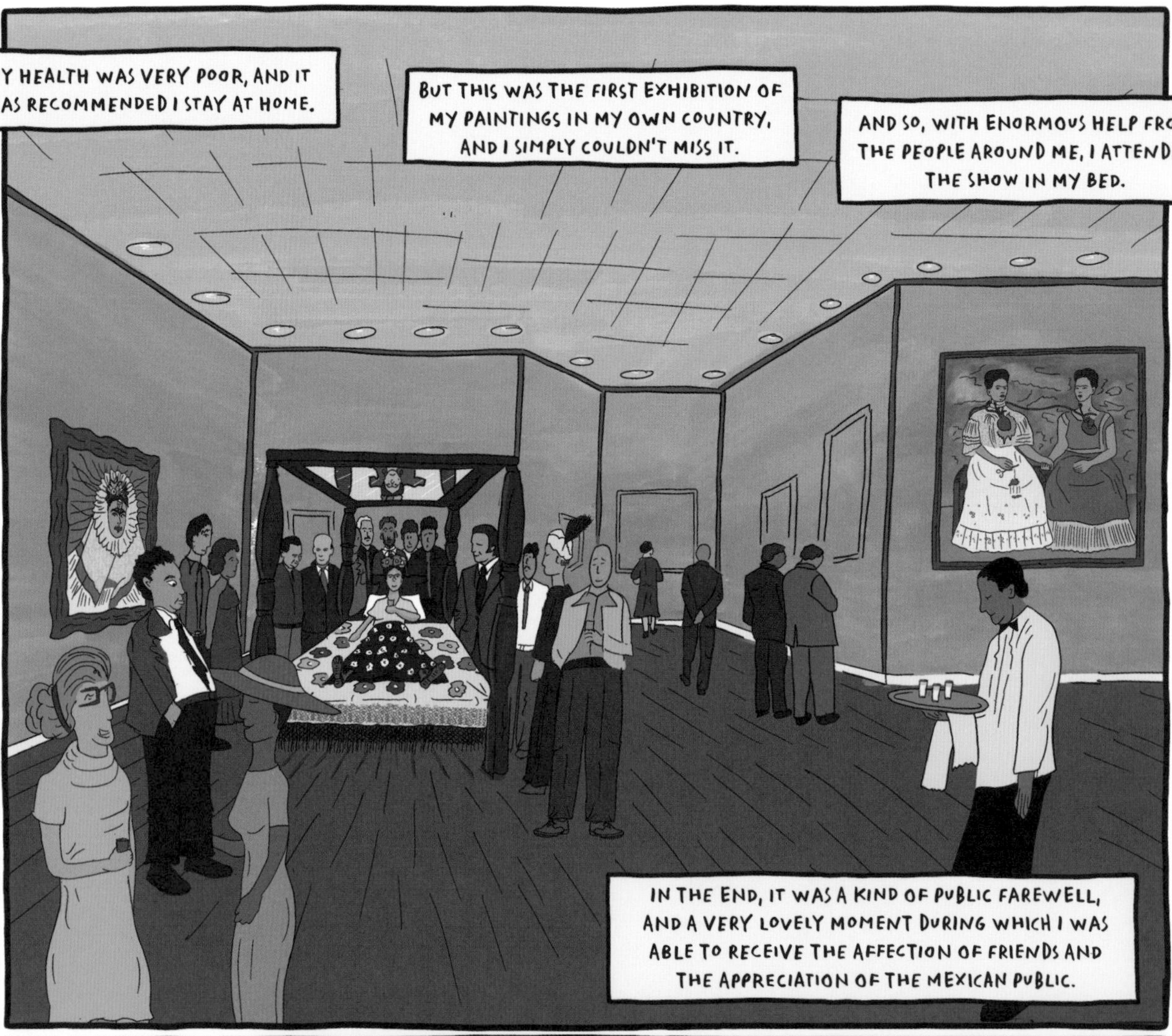
MY HEALTH WAS VERY POOR, AND IT WAS RECOMMENDED I STAY AT HOME.
BUT THIS WAS THE FIRST EXHIBITION OF MY PAINTINGS IN MY OWN COUNTRY, AND I SIMPLY COULDN'T MISS IT.
AND SO, WITH ENORMOUS HELP FROM THE PEOPLE AROUND ME, I ATTENDED THE SHOW IN MY BED.
IN THE END, IT WAS A KIND OF PUBLIC FAREWELL, AND A VERY LOVELY MOMENT DURING WHICH I WAS ABLE TO RECEIVE THE AFFECTION OF FRIENDS AND THE APPRECIATION OF THE MEXICAN PUBLIC.

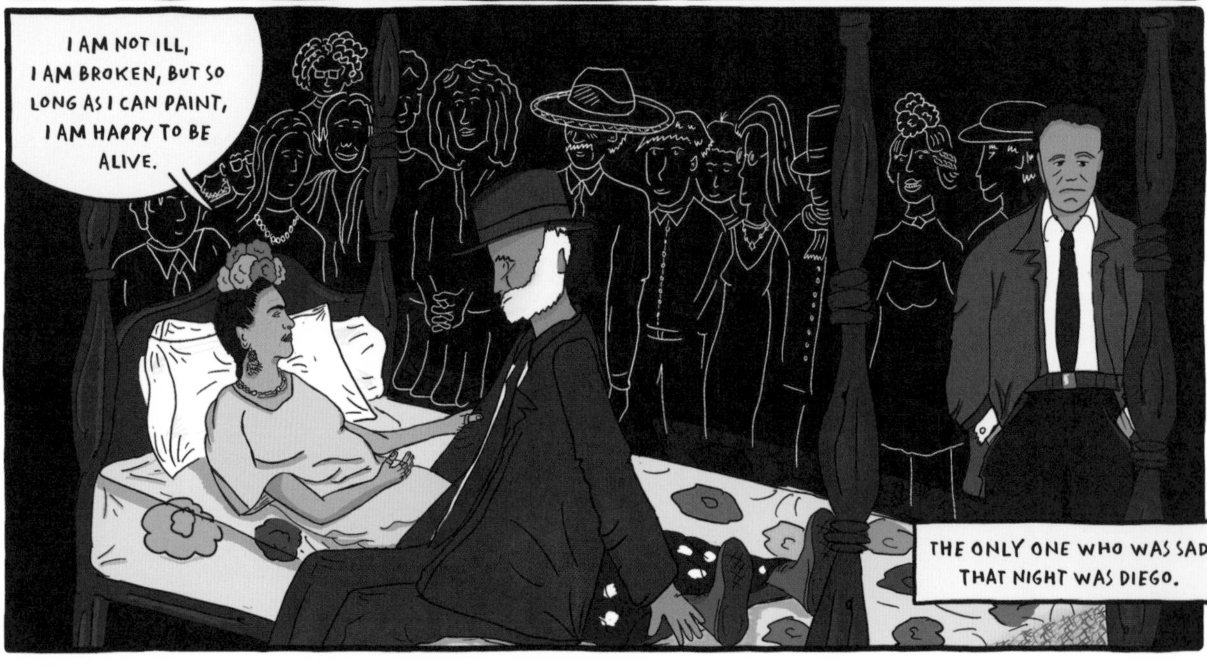
I AM NOT ILL, I AM BROKEN, BUT SO LONG AS I CAN PAINT, I AM HAPPY TO BE ALIVE.
THE ONLY ONE WHO WAS SAD THAT NIGHT WAS DIEGO.

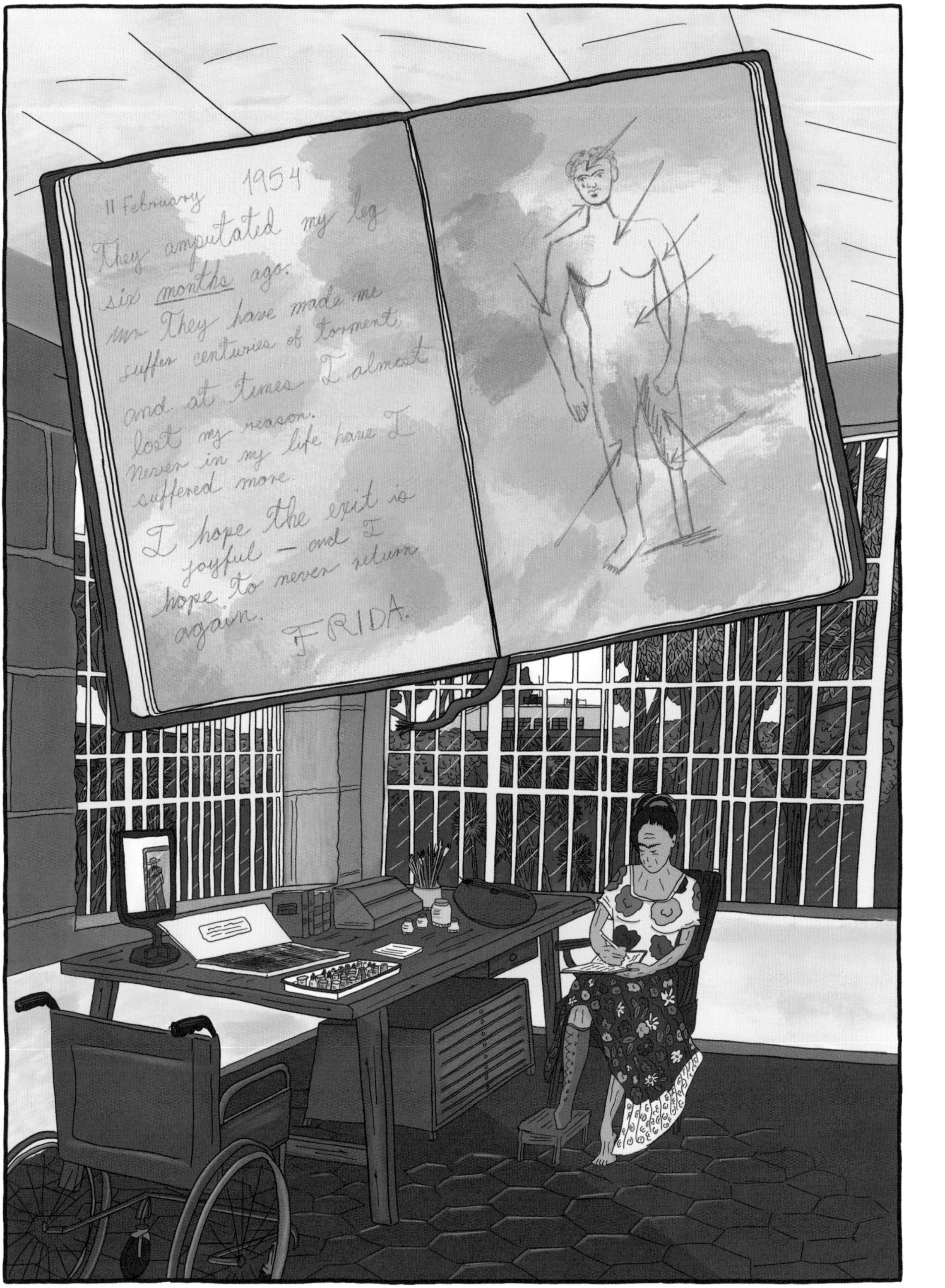
11 February 1954
They amputated my leg six months ago. They have made me suffer centuries of torment, and at times I almost lost my reason. Never in my life have I suffered more.
I hope the exit is joyful — and I hope to never return again.
FRIDA.

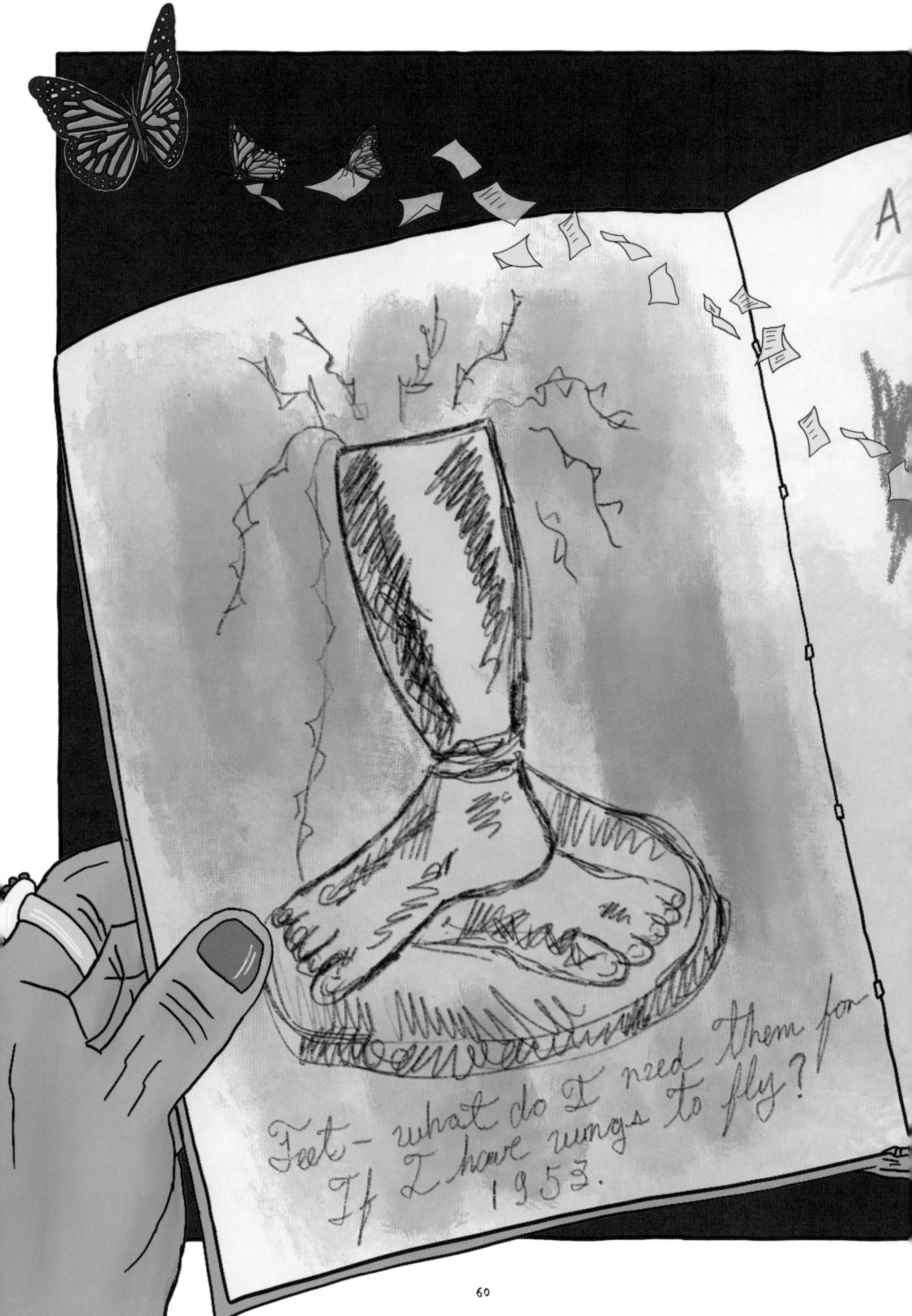
A
Feet- what do I need them for
If I have wings to fly?
1953.

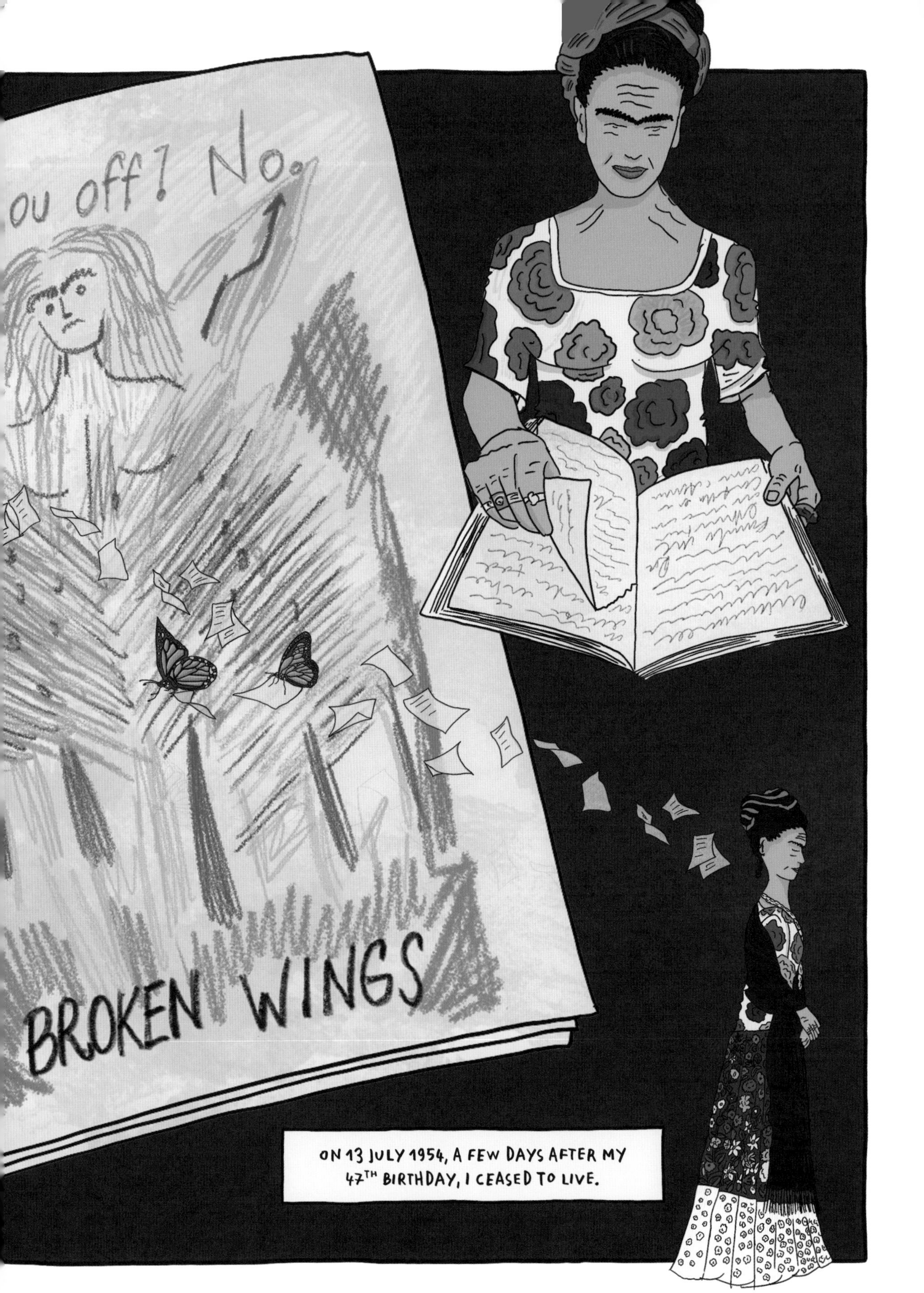
ou off? No.
BROKEN WINGS
ON 13 JULY 1954, A FEW DAYS AFTER MY 47TH BIRTHDAY, I CEASED TO LIVE.

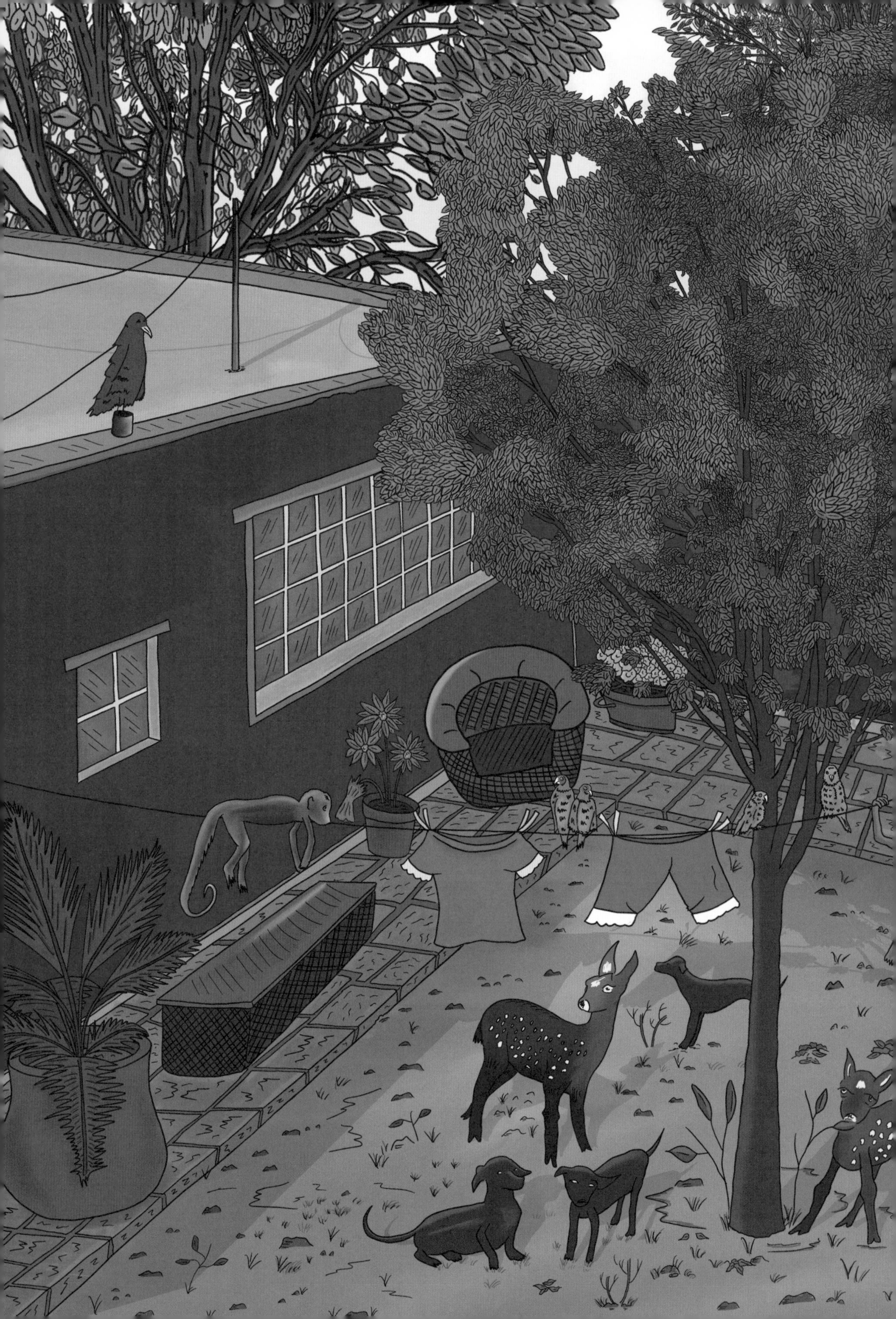

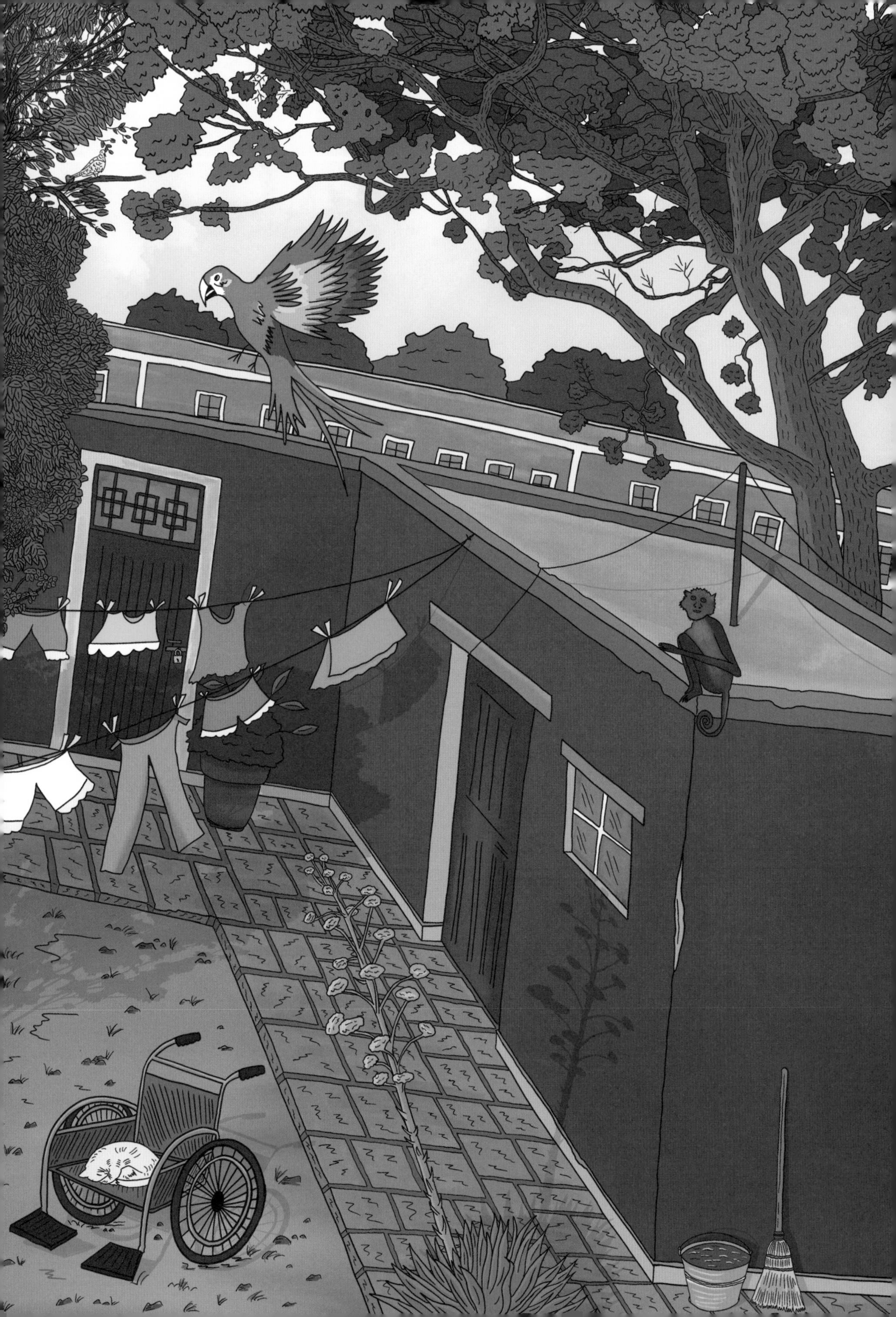

# FRIDA KAHLO (1907-1954)

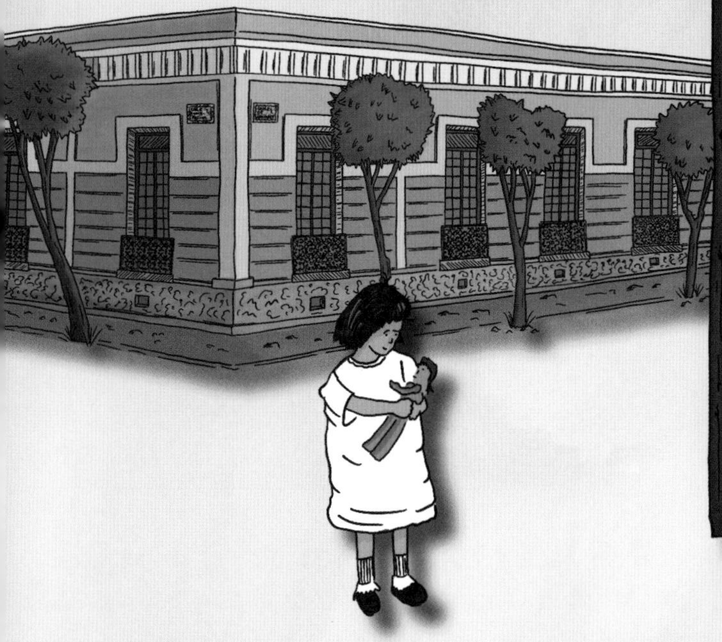

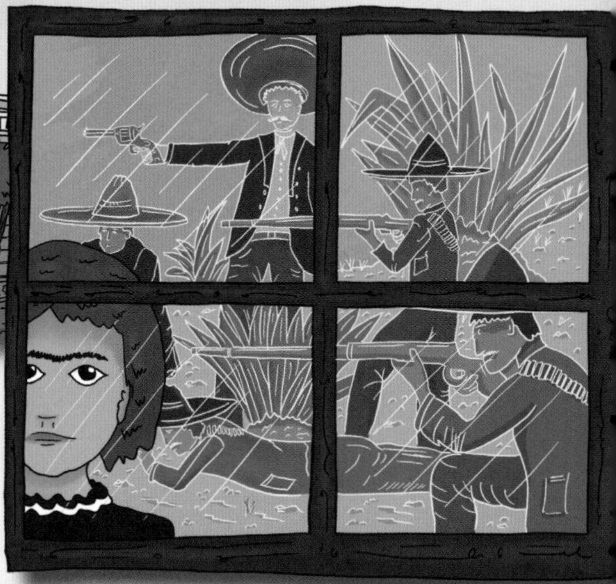

**1904**

Guillermo Kahlo (Frida's father) finishes building the family home in the district of Coyoacán.

**1907**

**6 July.** Frida Kahlo is born.

**1910**

**20 November.** The armed uprising known as the Mexican Revolution begins.

**1913**

**9 February.** The "Ten Tragic Days" begin.

Frida is diagnosed with poliomyelitis. (Other documentary evidence suggests she may have been 8 when she first fell ill.)

**1921**

**1921–1923.** Diego Rivera paints the mural "Creation" in the Simón Bolívar auditorium of the National Preparatory School.

Frida Kahlo first sets eyes on Diego Rivera at around this time.

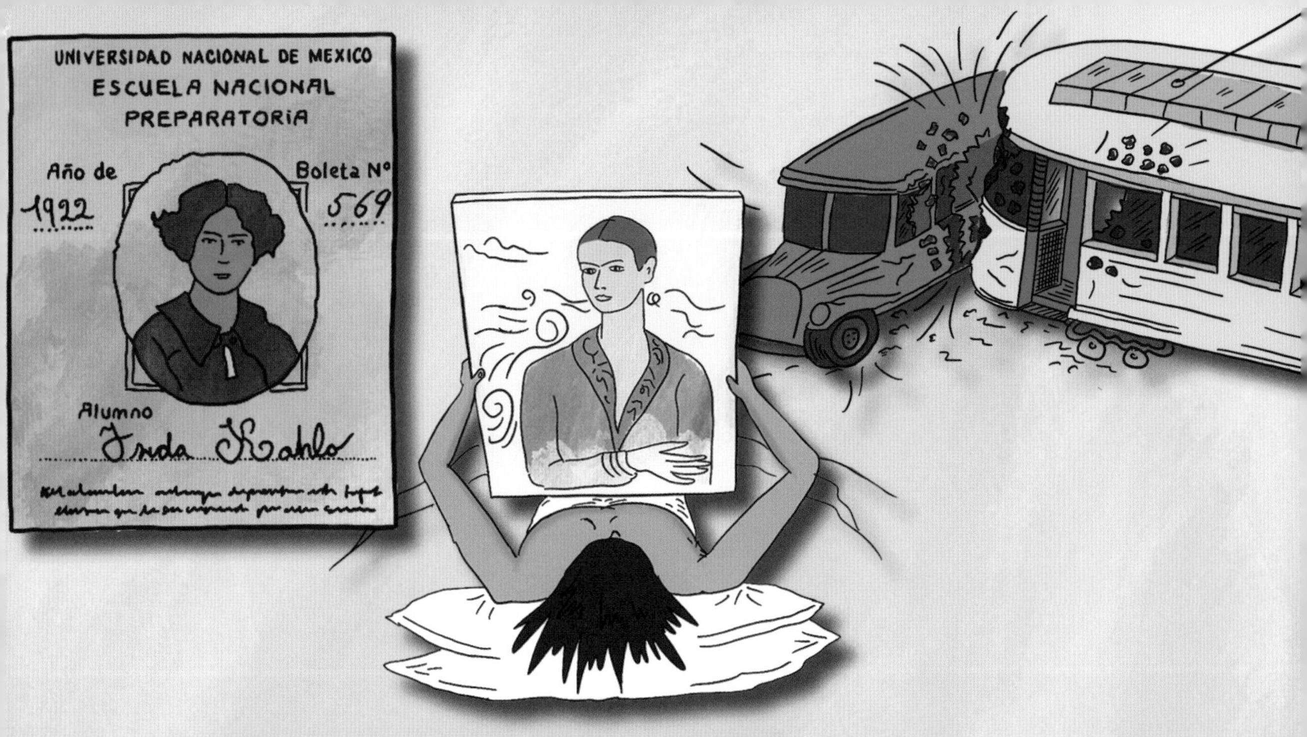
UNIVERSIDAD NACIONAL DE MEXICO
ESCUELA NACIONAL PREPARATORIA
Año de
1922
Boleta Nº
569
Alumno
Frida Kahlo

**1922**

Frida matriculates at the National Preparatory School.

**1923**

Frida begins a romantic relationship with Alejandro Gómez Arias.

**1925**

**17 September.** The bus in which Alejandro Gómez Arias and Frida Kahlo are travelling crashes.

Confined to bed because of the accident, Frida begins to paint on a regular basis.

**1926**

The first complications arising from Frida's injuries begin to appear. They will remain constant for the rest of her life.

**1928**

***Circa* 1928.** Frida visits Diego Rivera, then working on the murals of the Secretaría de Educación Pública building, and shows him her paintings.

| 1929 | 1930 | 1931 | 1932 | 1933 |
|------|------|------|------|------|

**21 August.**
Frida Kahlo and
Diego Rivera marry
in Coyoacán.

Frida and Diego live
for a time in
Cuernavaca,
while Rivera paints
a mural.

Frida suffers a
miscarriage.

**November.** Frida
and Diego travel
to New York.

Diego exhibits
his work in the
Museum of
Modern Art in
New York.

**21 April.** Frida and
Diego come to live
in Detroit.

**July**. Frida suffers
another miscarriage.

Matilde Calderón,
Frida's mother,
falls ill. Frida returns
to Mexico to be with her.

**15 September**. Matilde
Calderón dies.

**March.** Frida and
Diego return to New
York, where Diego
begins work on a mural
in the Rockefeller
Center.

**May.** Rivera's mural is
cancelled for including
the image of the
leader of the Russian
Revolution, Vladimir
Lenin.

**December.** Frida and
Diego return to live in
Mexico City, in their new
home in San Ángel.

Frida and Diego travel to
the United States, arriving
in San Francisco on 10
November.

Rivera paints the mural on
the city's Stock Exchange
building.

| 1934 | 1935 | 1936 | 1937 | 1938 |
|------|------|------|------|------|

André Breton visits Mexico and stays in the San Ángel house with Frida and Diego.

**February.** The mural of the Rockefeller Center is destroyed.

Diego embarks on an affair with Frida's sister Cristina.

Frida undergoes a third operation on her right foot, and spends some time in hospital.

**October.** Frida travels to New York.

**1 November.** Frida's solo exhibition at the Julien Levy gallery opens in New York.

Frida separates from Diego Rivera.

Frida has a romance with Isamu Noguchi.

**January.** Leon Trotsky and his wife, Natalia Sedova, take refuge in Mexico. They are sheltered in the Casa Azul of Coyoacán, where modifications are made to enhance the guests' security.

Frida has a romance with Leon Trotsky.

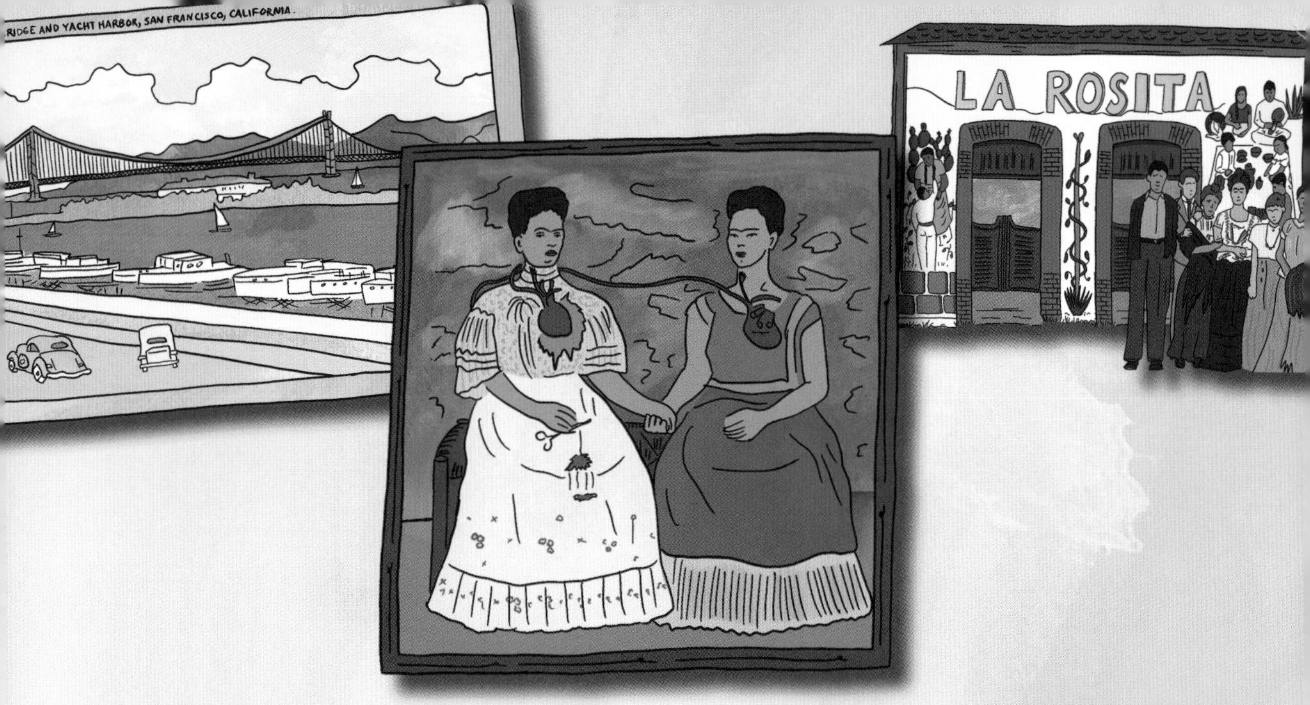
RIDGE AND YACHT HARBOR, SAN FRANCISCO, CALIFORNIA.
LA ROSITA

**1939**

Frida travels to France.

**10 March.** Frida takes part in the "Mexique" exhibition organized by André Breton. Frida meets, among others, Pablo Picasso Joan Miró Wassily Kandinsky Dora Maar Mary Reynolds Marcel Duchamp and Alice Rahon.

Frida and Diego divorce.

**1940**

Frida takes part in a group exhibition in the Arte Mexicano Gallery.

Trotsky is assassinated in his new residence in Coyoacán.

Frida travels to San Francisco to visit her doctor, Leo Eloesser.

Frida and Diego re-marry, this time in San Francisco.

"The Two Fridas" is exhibited at the Museum of Modern Art in New York.

**1941**

**14 April.** Guillermo Kahlo, Frida's father, dies.

**1942**

Frida exhibits her paintings in New York.

**1943**

Frida exhibits her paintings in Philadelphia.

Frida begins to teach classes at the La Esmeralda School of Art.

**19 June.** The murals of the Pulquería La Rosita tavern are unveiled – the work of a group of Frida's students known as "Los Fridos".

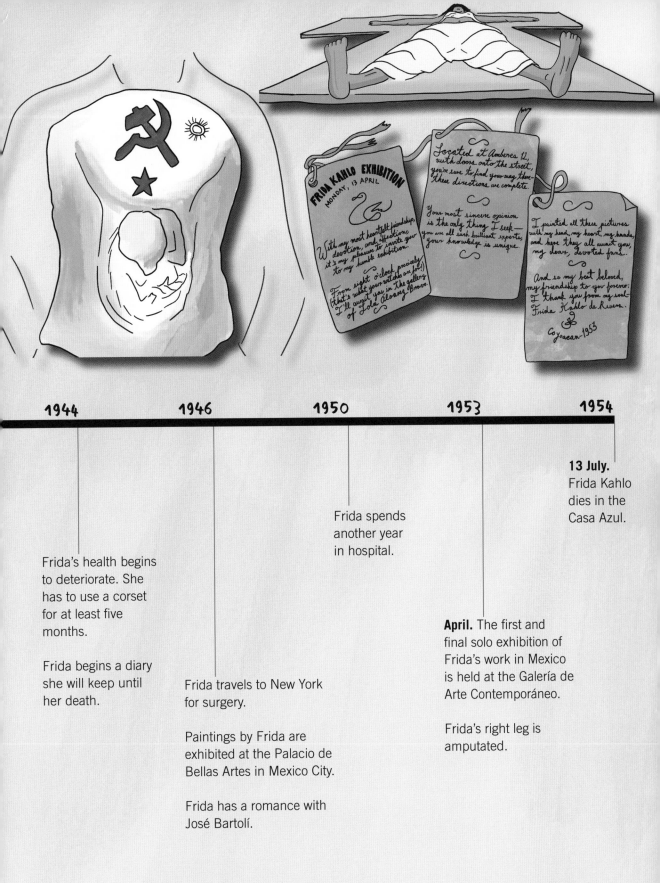

FRIDA KAHLO EXHIBITION
MONDAY, 13 APRIL
With my most heartfelt friendship, devotion, and affection, it's my pleasure to invite you to my humble exhibition.
From eight o'clock precisely (that's what your watches are for!) I'll await you in the gallery of Lola Álvarez Bravo.
Located at Amberes 12, with doors onto the street, you're sure to find your way there— these directions are complete.
Your most sincere opinion is the only thing I seek— you are all such brilliant experts, your knowledge is unique.
I painted all these pictures with my head, my heart, my hands, and here they all await you, my dear, devoted fans.
And so my best beloved, my friendship to you forever: I thank you from my soul— Frida Kahlo de Rivera.
Coyoacan-1953

**1944**

Frida's health begins to deteriorate. She has to use a corset for at least five months.

Frida begins a diary she will keep until her death.

**1946**

Frida travels to New York for surgery.

Paintings by Frida are exhibited at the Palacio de Bellas Artes in Mexico City.

Frida has a romance with José Bartolí.

**1950**

Frida spends another year in hospital.

**1953**

**April.** The first and final solo exhibition of Frida's work in Mexico is held at the Galería de Arte Contemporáneo.

Frida's right leg is amputated.

**1954**

**13 July.** Frida Kahlo dies in the Casa Azul.

**Bibliography**


*Diario de Frida Kahlo* (La Vaca Independiente, 1995)

*Querido Doctorcito: Frida Kahlo–Leo Eloesser: Correspondencia* (DGE Equilibrista, 2007)

Hayden Herrera, *Frida: una biografía de Frida Kahlo* (Taurus, 2019)

Margaret Hooks, *Frida Kahlo: la gran ocultadora* (Turner, 2002)

Graciela Iturbide, *Demerol: El baño de Frida Kahlo* (Editorial RM, 2009)

Isolda Pinedo Kahlo, *Frida íntima* (Ediciones Dipon / Ediciones Gato Azul, 2019)

Pablo Ortiz Monasterio, *Frida Kahlo, sus fotos* (Editorial RM, 2010)

Manuel González Ramírez, *Recuerdos de un preparatoriano de siempre* (Universidad Nacional Autónoma de México, 1982)

Claire Wilcox and Circe Henestrosa, *Frida Kahlo: Making Herself Up* (Victoria and Albert Museum, 2018)

Bertram D. Wolfe, *La fabulosa vida de Diego Rivera* (Diana, 1986)


**Notes**

The cover illustration is based on two paintings: *Self-Portrait with Thorn Necklace and Hummingbird*, 1940, and *My Grandparents, My Parents, and I (Family Tree)*, 1936.

The letters on pages 27 and 43 replicate extracts from Frida Kahlo's letters, but are not exact transcripts.

The first drawing on page 34 was inspired by an original painting by Miguel Covarrubias.

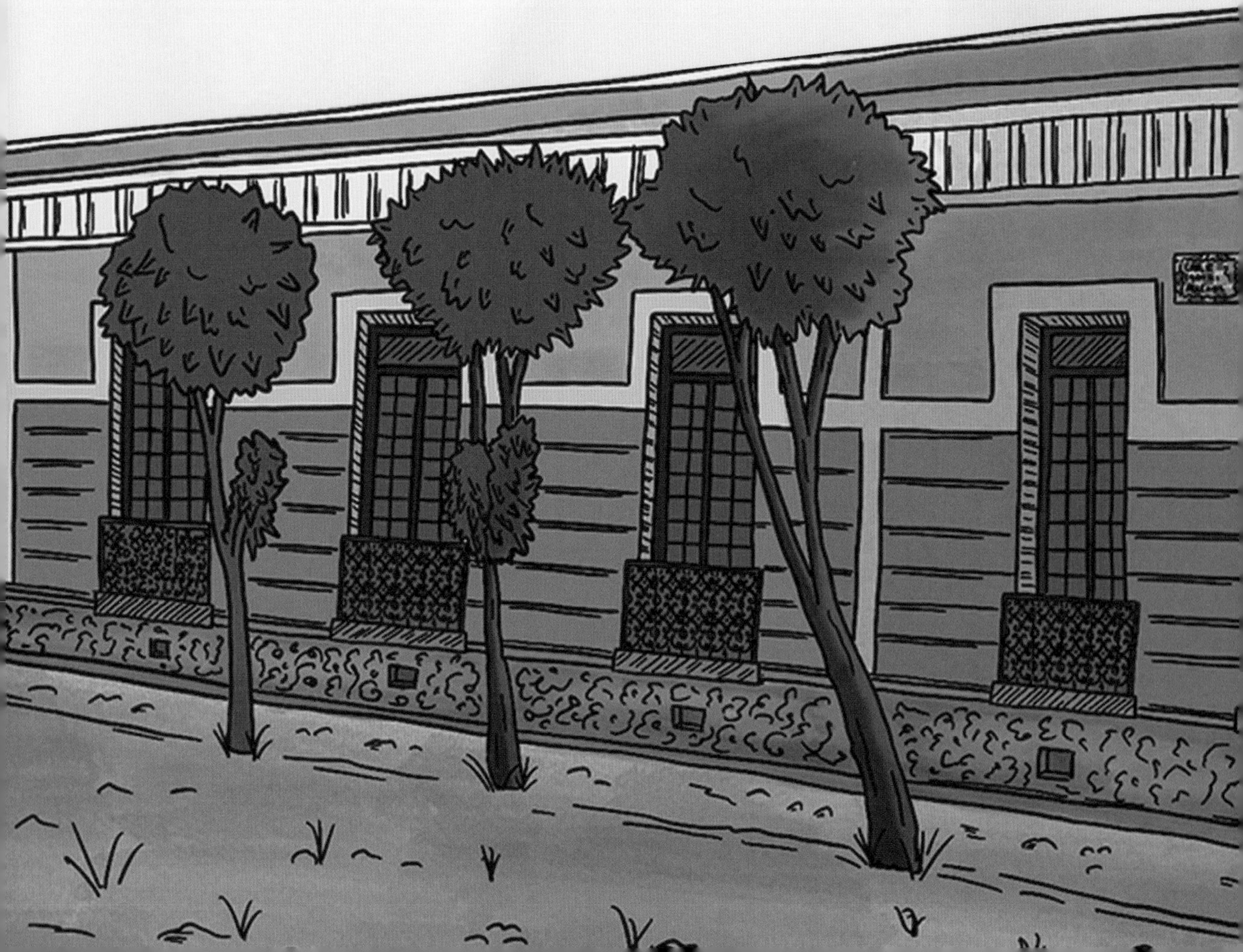

**Acknowledgements**

A very special thanks to:

Sara Alfonso, for her powerful insights, and all her hard work behind this book.
Emma Hayley, for helping me achieve the true potential of each of its images.
Carlos Phillips, for helping and believing in us.
Perla Labarthe, for opening the doors of the Casa Azul for us, and for all her help.
Xochiquetzal González, for going over the scripts and sketches, and for her astute corrections.
Irene de la Mora, for being the first reader of this book, and for imagining every panel.
Ana Mauer, for reading the story, and helping me understand how to tell it.
Circe Henestrosa, for the beautiful foreword and all the little details she helped me to correct.

And to Daniela Rocha, for all those hours talking about Frida (and the *gordito*), and her infinite help in this adventure of drawing stories.

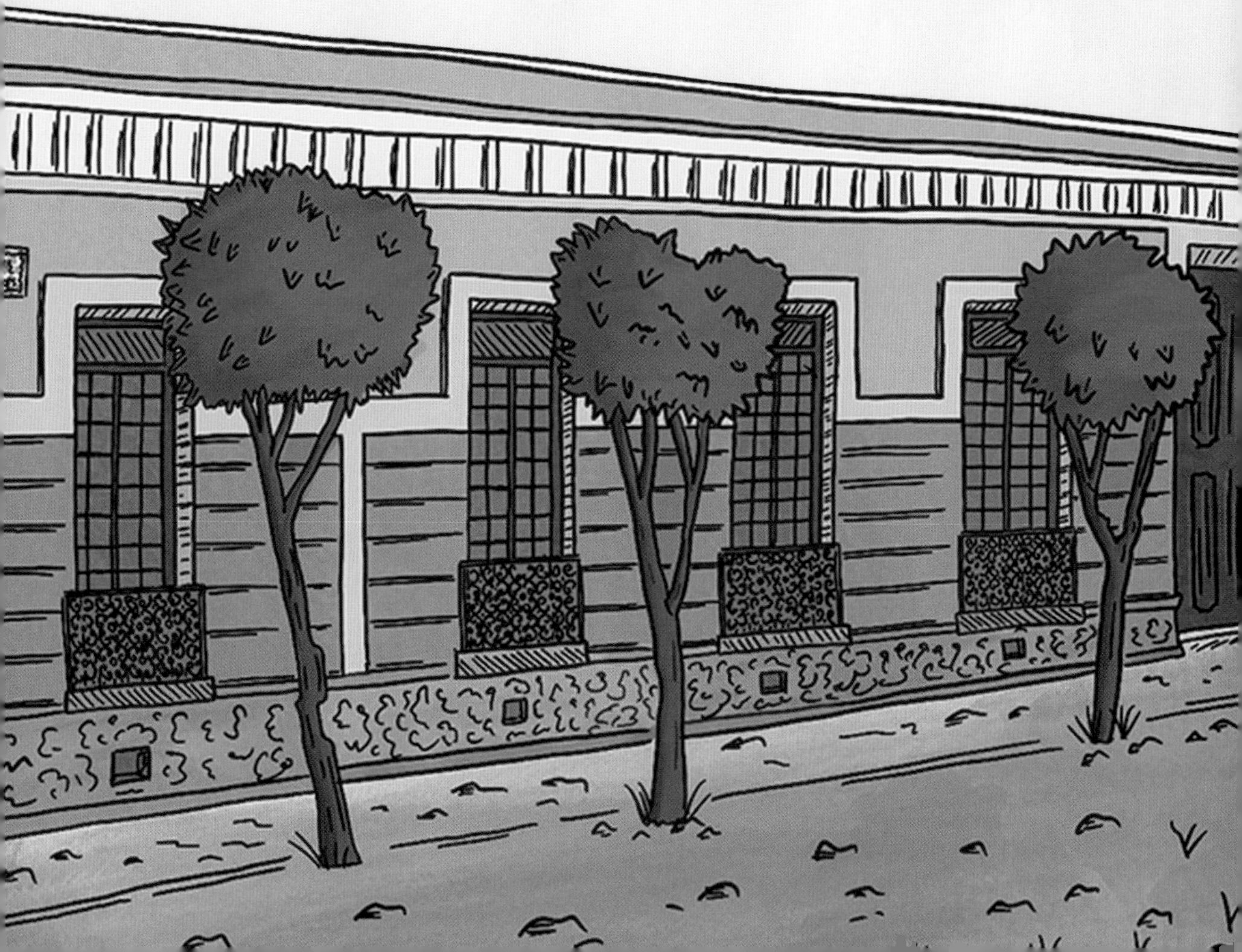

THIS BOOK WAS FIRST PRINTED IN 2023,
IN THE 116TH ANNIVERSARY OF
FRIDA'S BIRTH

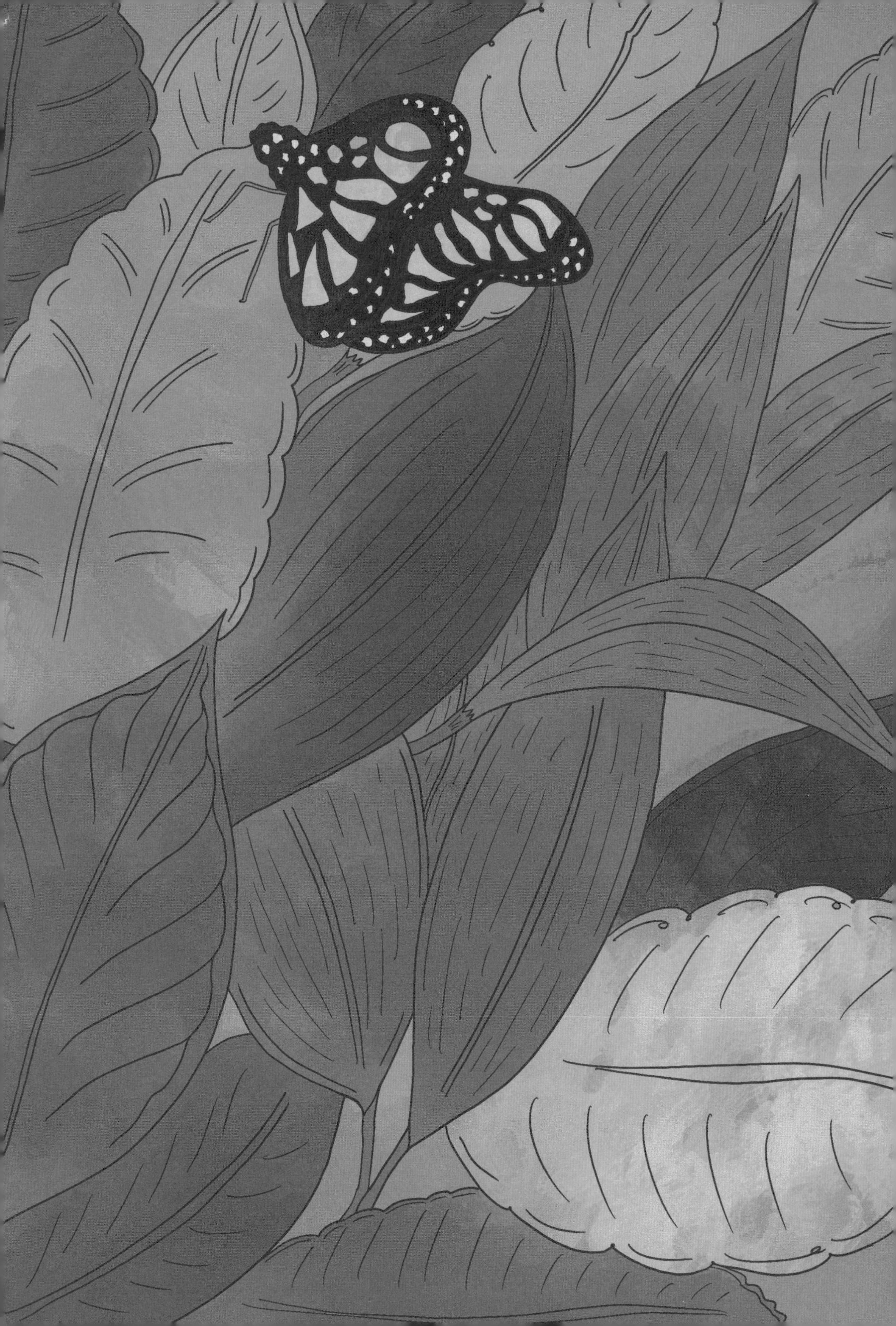

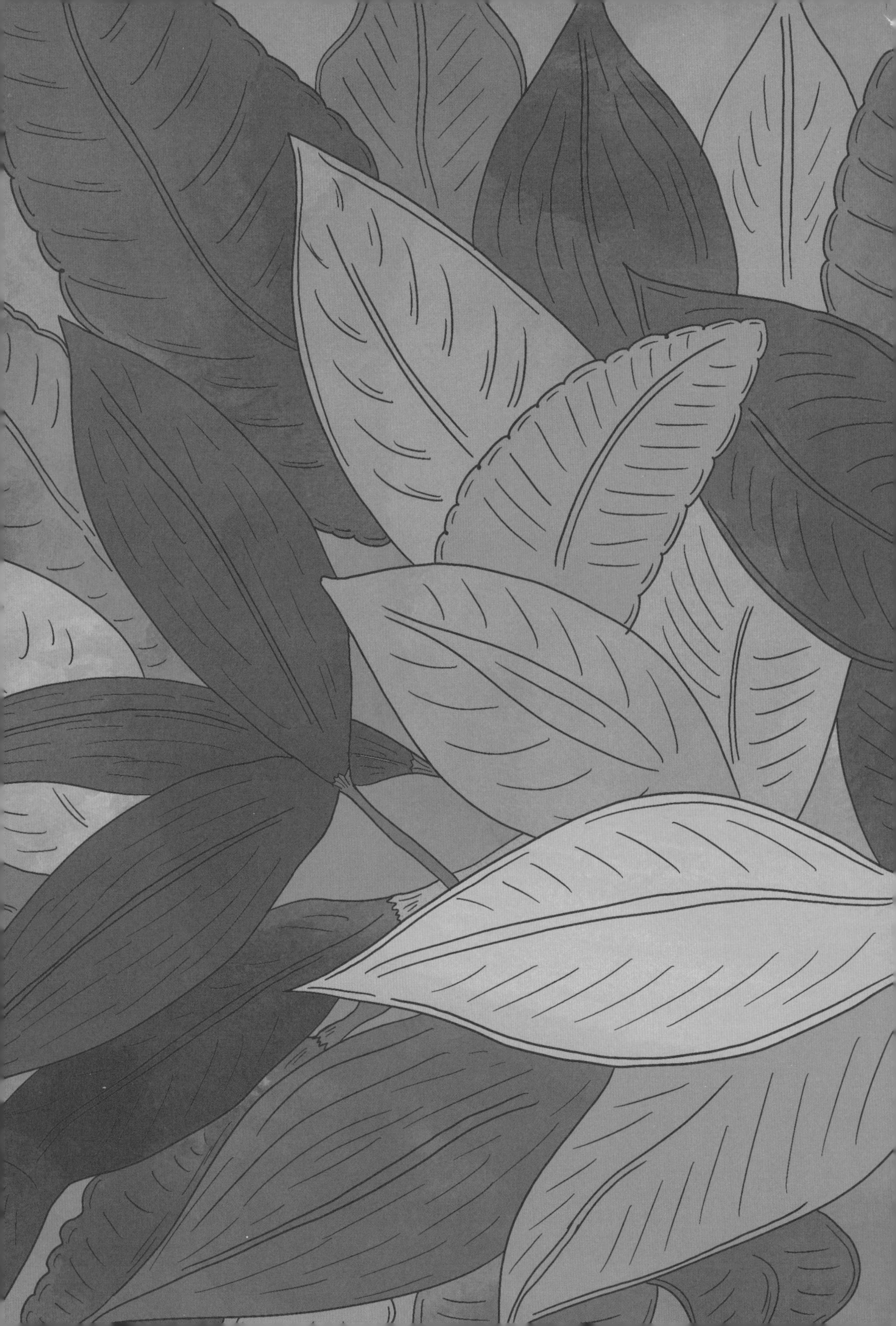